Women Through Our Eyes

Midwives Share Their Stories

By

Pamela S. F. Glenn, CNM

And

Margaret A. Taylor, CNM

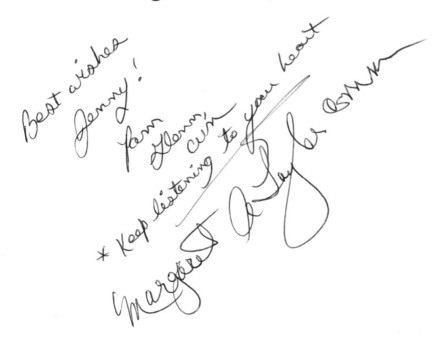

Best wishes Jenny!

From Glenn CNM

* Keep listening to your heart

Margaret A Taylor CNM

Dedication

We dedicate this book to the midwives who shared their stories with us and provided a unique glimpse into the lives of women.

Acknowledgements

We would like to acknowledge the phenomenal women whose life experiences led to the stories in this collection. It is you for whom we have the utmost respect and admiration and who inspire us all. It is important to also thank the many friends, family, and peers who supported us with the multitude of edits to this book, providing endless encouragement for its completion.

CONTENTS

CONTENTS

Introduction

Maybe we were delusional from the afternoon Palm Desert sun as we took a break from our midwife convention. Our conversation ended with the following conclusion: "We have such a unique perspective of women's lives from the work we do. We really need to gather these stories and share them with others!" This discussion sparked the flame that blazed our commitment to this book. Lunch was placed before us but we hardly saw the food. Instead, all we could see were the rich tales that filled each midwife's heart. We were surrounded by the legends of our profession who for decades believed fervently in midwifery and fought battle after battle to bring our profession to women. As always, they so graciously made themselves available to others. These dynamic pioneers willingly shared their knowledge, their vast experiences, and most striking to us, their stories. Also present were midwives who, like us, continued to work "in the trenches" acquiring vast hands-on experiences as they cared for women from all walks of life. Strenuous hours did not deter their fierce commitment to being "with women," the Latin definition of "midwife." And of course there were the students, always energetic and hungry to follow their calling and join these professional ranks.

Many breakfasts and coffee house conversations later, our goal was narrowed down: We wanted to gather the stories of women–women who inspired midwives, women who overcame tremendous obstacles to find their true voice, women who provided us with extraordinary life lessons. It is important to clarify this is *not* simply a collection of birth stories. Rather, these are portraits of women through a tale about their lives. While birth may be included in some of the stories, it is not the focus of this book. Just like our profession, it is so much more.

You may be asking, what exactly *is* midwifery and how is it so much more? Traditionally midwives have provided health services through pregnancy, labor, birth, and postpartum. In addition, however, we care for women throughout all the phases of their lives. From annual exams, birth control visits, sexually transmitted infection (STI) checks, perimenopause education, and a variety of other issues, midwifery takes women's health to a whole new level. Our practice approach assesses the whole woman. This includes her unique history, her emotional well-being, her support system, her spirituality, and her cultural background and beliefs.

We listen and learn from our patients. A connection forms. A bond develops. Women often identify us by saying, "That's my midwife." They know we are there for them. As a result we are witness to their lives, their courage, their stamina and guts, and their humor. Capturing the essence of these powerful qualities in women from our unique perspective has been the ultimate purpose of this writing project.

We interviewed midwives from across the country, from a vast array of backgrounds, and from students ready to practice as well as midwives ready to retire. They openly shared their stories with us. In time our interviews became more focused, our writing more fluent, and our editing more decisive. It has been a long and arduous process, but also fruitful and fulfilling. The art of writing came alive as we did our best to paint the words onto paper and accurately portray each woman's portrait.

Along the way, we made a wonderful, serendipitous discovery. Each midwife had her *own* unique story to tell–the journey which led her to listen to her soul and choose this profession. Thus, not only do we have stories of women as told by their midwives, but we've also included a few of the personal tales of the midwives themselves. We believe these extra narratives add a rich dimension and substance to the book

Names and identifying circumstances have been changed for every midwife and character described so as to provide anonymity. Likewise, creative liberties were taken to fully develop each story. To all of you who shared your stories and experienced them firsthand, you know who you are: brave, courageous beyond imagination, strong as ever, and an inspiration for us all.

Listening to these tales affected us deeply and kept us ever committed to this book. The revelations from their insights and experiences became a part of our own personal lives. Coincidentally their voices and inspirational quotes often came alive as we, the authors, faced our own challenges day to day.

The midwives who were interviewed were also impacted by the process. Pure joy radiated from them as they shared the events that led them to this profession. The interview also provided them the opportunity to examine their own past journey. As they retraced their steps with us, it became apparent that their lives had been greatly enriched by their work. A spirit of accomplishment came over them as they examined their service to women. Likewise, as interviewers, we became acutely aware of our role as listeners, providing the midwives with the gift of validation for their numerous contributions.

To conclude, women everywhere will identify with the stories in *Women Through Our Eyes.* This book presents the stories of phenomenal, yet everyday women. It provides the exceptional perspective acquired by midwives who care for women throughout their lives.

Pamela S. F. Glenn, CNM, MS
Margaret A. Taylor, CNM, MS, FACNM

Disclaimer: It is important to acknowledge that although you may relate to the clinical situations described in this book, it is not to be used as a clinical resource. For any health questions or medical concerns, please consult your health care provider. Thank you.

Our suggestions for reading this book

How do we recommend you read this book? However you wish. Read one story at a time or cover to cover in a single sitting. You may discover it is best to read a single portrait and then contemplate its message for your life. Or, if you prefer, read one full chapter at a time before taking time to pause and reflect.

You can take this book one step further. Share it with the other significant people in your life. Give it as a gift to your mother, your sister, your girlfriends or co-workers. Or better yet, share it with the men in your life who do not often get the opportunity to have this unique insight into the opposite sex that this book offers.

Use this collection of stories to bring people together—either one-on-one or with a colorful, eclectic gathering. Share your thoughts about how these portraits have impacted you personally. Pick the one character you could most closely identify with. Which story touched your heart the deepest? Which one made you laugh and which one made you cry? Which one hit the nail on the head with its message for your life? Be brave and share your own life stories that come to mind. Be brutally honest. Pave the way for others to respond truthfully in return. These writings can be the springboard to more intimate conversations, to deeper reflections, and to an enhanced understanding of one another. And, listen to their responses. You may be blown away by the personal experiences that others share with you!

Pamela S. F. Glenn, CNM, MS
Margaret A. Taylor, CNM, MS, FACNM

Chapter 1: Life Priorities

We all have a set of priorities that gives focus to our lives. We may not always recognize what our specific priorities are until confronted with a circumstance that forces a decision. In this chapter we will see how priorities kick in from deep within the soul and, as a result, drive each of us to determine our own destiny.

The Birth-Day Gift

Elizabeth weighs a patient's demand for pain medication, not knowing if it will fit with her usual labor management style in rural America.

Mary was a farmer's wife in her early thirties, dress size fourteen, and mother of four. Mary was no beauty queen. Her dark brown hair was cut short for easy maintenance. She didn't have time for makeup. In addition to child care and housework, Mary helped with the farm, feeding pigs and hauling grain. She was a strong, down-to-earth wife and mother, a no-nonsense woman.

Mary was an amazing mother. She knew how to have babies and take care of kids. Baby number five was on the way. Knowing this was going to be her last baby, she had just one request for this labor.

"I want pain medication," she told me. "I want Nubain. Ten milligrams."

Surprised by her comment, I tried a diplomatic approach. "I'm not opposed to using pain medication in labor if it's needed, Mary. How about if we wait and see?"

Mary was adamant. "I'm not trying to get rid of all the pain with that epidural-thing. I just want to take an edge off the contractions and have a little more control."

Back in my office I updated Mary's prenatal record, making a note of her request while pondering the pros and cons of Nubain. When given intravenously, this narcotic works within a couple minutes and its relaxing effects can last a couple hours. However Nubain can also make newborns sluggish, especially if a fast labor doesn't allow enough time for the drug to clear from their systems. The baby could end up having a slow heart rate and difficulty breathing at birth. While reviewing Mary's previous labor records, I noted that she delivered her babies quickly, all the more reason her request had me concerned.

Pain medication remained Mary's main focus at each subsequent prenatal visit, no matter how much evidence I presented regarding the benefits of holding off on this option.

12

"Elizabeth, this is my fifth baby. I know exactly what I want," she insisted. Then Mary looked into my eyes and pounded her fist on the desk with each word: "I want that drug!"

I responded with concern, "What if there's no time to give you the drug? If we administer the medication too close to the delivery, the baby might get too much of it in his system and could have trouble breathing."

"Elizabeth, it'll all work out. You don't need to worry about a thing," Mary affirmed.

I finally acquiesced, "All right. Let's see how it goes."

When Mary went into labor two days before her due date, she called me at home. "Elizabeth, it's starting. I'm not quite ready to come to the hospital, but I want you to be ready for me."

"Okay," I answered. "I'll be waiting for your next call. About how close are your contractions?"

"Oh, they're about six to eight minutes–oops! Well, darn. My water just broke. I'd better head on over." We both knew her labor would move much faster now.

Her piercing glare greeted me in the birthing room. "Elizabeth, give me the drug."

"Let's first see how you're doing," I stalled, watching her breathe through the next contraction. "Mary, you're doing so well." After the next contraction I continued to encourage her, "You're doing just great. You're in control." A sweep of the birthing room showed me that everything was set up for the birth. I reinforced her breathing efforts. "Excellent job."

But with the next contraction Mary grabbed my lab coat and demanded, "It might look good to you, Elizabeth, but I want that medication and need it now. I'm not in this for a medal."

I relented and ordered half of the regular dose with instructions to the nurse to keep the remaining medication ready. The nurse injected her with the smaller amount.

13

Mary's cervix was almost fully dilated, typically not the time to administer this drug. "Surely she'll be ready to push the baby out momentarily," I rationalized.

But after ten more contractions, she declared, "You didn't give me enough. It wasn't enough!"

Just then I realized Mary was literally hanging onto the baby until she got the birth experience she wanted. I nodded to the nurse who gave her the other half of the medication.

She responded with a heavy sigh, closed her eyes, and relaxed. "That's exactly what I needed." Ten minutes later Mary pushed out her last baby. Her exuberant boy was born without any visible impact from the Nubain. She smiled.

Mary knew exactly what she wanted for her last birth–a little less pain, a little more control. It was a birth-day gift she was determined to give herself. And she did.

I'm a Wreck. How Are You?

Stephanie, a premenopausal midwife, urgently prioritizes health concerns with her perimenopausal patient.

"Stephanie, I feel like an absolute wreck!" Martha proclaimed, even though she had never met me. "I think I might be going through menopause, but I'm not sure. All of these weird sensations are driving me crazy!" Martha rolled her eyes and drew circles in the air with her fingers. "You know," she added in a higher octave, "I truly believe I'm going nutso!"

We laughed together. However, despite Martha's wonderful sense of humor, I knew this was no laughing matter. "Okay, let's go through each symptom one at a time," I suggested. Martha immediately listed her most pressing concerns, from hot flashes and night sweats to irregular periods. She complained of moodiness and was having trouble concentrating.

I took lengthy notes and asked many detailed questions. "When did all this start? Do you get hot flashes every night? Are you able to get back to sleep after they happen?" Martha identified major disruptions with her sleep followed by fatigue each day.

Before launching into my list of suggestions, I asked one more question. "By the way, how would you describe your relationship with your husband Jim through all of this?"

Martha paused and then explained he hadn't been quite himself lately. "It's been a stressful time for both of us," she admitted. "Me, with all my crazy menopausal hormone changes. But for Jim it's been tough for other reasons. In just the past year he lost his father to cancer. His best friend died of a sudden heart attack. And then our future son-in-law died in a car crash. That boy was like a son to Jim." Martha stopped talking for a moment and then quietly shared, "You know, it was the strangest thing the other day. Jim came into the kitchen and said to me, 'Don't worry, hon. I don't have any thoughts of killing myself or anything like that.'"

15

Without thinking my words rushed out, "He said *what?*" My pen stopped moving. I looked into her eyes. My voice softened. "I'm really concerned about what you just told me, Martha. Hearing a statement like that makes me wonder if your husband has been thinking about killing himself. It's a red flag. He may be sending out a warning with his words."

Second-guessing myself for a moment, it remained clear this situation needed to be addressed. I asked Martha more directly, "Did you happen to ask Jim if he was suicidal?"

"No," Martha answered. Her eye brows rose as she considered the question. "It never even crossed my mind."

A wave of urgency suddenly flowed through every cell of my body. I knew we had a lot to address with Martha's symptoms, but her husband's situation took over as my new focus. "Look Martha, I'm going to be extremely blunt here. I agree you *are* a perimenopausal wreck." I paused and smiled. She chuckled softly. "I'm here to help you address all of your issues. But first, we need to get Jim some help immediately. This is serious and it's urgent."

Martha listened attentively. I repeated my concern that Jim may be suicidal and added that the circumstances of the past year made it more likely. I kept hoping my words were getting through to her. My voice grew in intensity. "He needs to see a professional therapist right away. Go home. Talk with him. Call this mental health number to get some help. Encourage him to get an appointment today. And most importantly, do not take 'no' for an answer."

Martha looked stunned, but nodded her head and agreed with the plan. "I will, Stephanie," she responded, as if all the puzzle pieces of Jim's life over the past year were suddenly falling into place.

"Please call me later and let me know how it goes, okay?"

She nodded repeatedly, almost robotically, not saying another word.

"Here's my direct phone number." Martha clenched the paper in her hand and headed out the door. I watched her leave. This woman who initially entered the clinic looking frazzled and desperate now walked out briskly, her eyes focused forward, as if on a military mission. Martha showed an amazing ability to put

16

aside her own overwhelming concerns to focus on the more immediate needs of her husband. She was probably experiencing some shock. "And the same goes for me," I realized, never imagining the need to prioritize a situation like this.

While sitting at my desk waiting to see the next patient, I worried about Jim. The warning signs of suicide were clear–the tragic losses, the change in Jim's demeanor, and his statement to Martha in the kitchen. It rattled me to realize how easily this could have been missed. It was a reminder of how important it was to listen and pick up on cues.

Later that afternoon the phone rang at my desk. I heard Martha's voice. "Jim has agreed to go for help," she announced. "We already have an appointment this evening." I sighed with relief.

A couple weeks later Martha returned for her follow-up appointment. She was very talkative, but not about any of her original complaints. Instead, Martha talked about Jim. "I can already see a difference in him," she described. "He is getting better each day and continues to go to counseling." Martha went on to explain, "We had a long talk the other night. Jim admitted to me that he was having suicidal thoughts. And I had no idea, absolutely no clue at all." Then Martha added, "Stephanie, thank you for catching this. I don't know what would have happened if you hadn't been so tuned-in."

We both paused before proceeding to Martha's perimenopausal concerns. My mind replayed the chain of events that led to this moment of relief and peace. Thank goodness I asked Martha about Jim during that initial visit. And it was so fortunate she shared his unusual statement with me. It was inspirational to have witnessed Martha's keen ability to quickly readjust her priorities under these unique circumstances.

The crisis had passed. Jim was healing. And Martha was now ready to address her own problems–not as a perimenopausal wreck but as a woman transformed and on a new mission.

Doing This My Way

Veronica is the primary nurse-midwife in an inner-city clinic for teens and regularly encounters young women in crisis. One remarkable client stands out with a very determined spirit.

Tonisha slumped in the exam room chair with her chin on her chest. With pursed lips she wrapped her arms around herself as if she were wearing a straightjacket. At sixteen years old, Tonisha suspected she was pregnant. Her rounded abdomen told me the lab tests were unnecessary. My routine exam confirmed the diagnosis.

"I'm pregnant, ain't I?" Tonisha took a deep breath.

"You certainly are," I replied.

Tonisha turned her head away and exhaled a profanity.

I clarified, "Just about sixteen weeks along. Go ahead and get dressed. I'll be back in a few minutes and we can talk about your options."

I closed the door and breathed my own heavy sigh and silent curse. "Why don't these kids just use birth control?" After making a few notes on Tonisha's chart I prepared myself for that inevitable conversation.

Reentering the room, Tonisha blurted out, "I'm gonna have this baby even if Marcus don't want it. I ain't havin' no abortion like my sista. I already love this baby and can be a good mom!"

I blinked a couple times and swallowed my shock. "You've made a firm decision?"

"Yeah, I have," she affirmed.

"All right then," I responded, "Here's how you can be a good mom starting today."

Tonisha listened carefully as I explained the importance of regular clinic visits and good nutrition. We even began talking about the labor and birth process. While reviewing everything from prenatal vitamins to parenting skills, Tonisha questioned it all to make sure she understood. I had never seen a teenager set such clear-cut goals for motherhood this early in her pregnancy.

18

All pregnant teens at the clinic were seen by Kathryn, our social worker. When I told her about Tonisha, she just shrugged, saying, "We'll see if she really follows through."

Over the next five months, Tonisha came to her clinic appointments faithfully. Each visit confirmed her baby was growing and the heart beat was strong. I praised her efforts to eat the right foods and gain the right amount of weight. She simply grinned.

At the end of her seventh appointment, it was time to talk to Tonisha about her specific plans for labor and birth. She was adjusting her shirt over the protruding basketball of her belly with a tender caress when I returned to the exam room. She turned her cautious eyes to me and started the conversation. "Well, I wanna have this baby before my due date. And I'm gonna do it all natural, ya know."

I suppressed a chuckle and raised an inquisitive eyebrow. "Okay, what does 'all natural' mean to you, Tonisha?"

"I don't wanna have no pain killers. I figured if Mary can do it with Jesus, then I can do it for my baby."

I was getting used to Tonisha's assertions and managed to maintain my composure. "Interesting, but 2000 years ago, Mary didn't have the options that are available today."

"I ain't havin' no needle in my back if that's what you're talkin' 'bout," Tonisha's eyes were open wide.

"An epidural isn't exactly what I meant," I explained. "But it is a pain relief method that we have today. Sometimes women who don't intend to have painkillers change their minds during labor. It's important you know about all of your options."

"Well, I'm not taking nothin'," emphasized Tonisha, crossing her arms tightly. "And another thing, I don't need none of them birthin' classes."

I smiled, thinking about how many women had told me that same thing. "Tonisha, learning about what will happen to your body during labor will help you understand all the sensations you'll be experiencing. The classes will also give

19

you some great tips to help you through this experience, especially since you want to avoid medication."

"Can't I just learn it from you?" she requested. "School makes it hard to get to them classes. And I gotta work at the grocery store. I gotta get some money for this baby." We talked through a plan to go over labor and birth topics during the next few prenatal visits and added some time to her appointments. She agreed to it all.

"Okay, Tonisha. You are astonishing," I replied after working out the details with her. She grinned again.

In the middle of the night, December 12, the midwife on-call phoned to let me know Tonisha was in labor at the hospital. I shook my head in amazement. It was two weeks before her due date.

At the hospital, I changed into scrub clothes and headed for the birthing unit. The midwife who admitted Tonisha reported on the night's events. "She came in at about midnight and was almost four centimeters dilated. I just checked her a couple minutes ago and she's already progressed nicely to six. Her contractions are now coming every two to three minutes. She's tired but coping very well. You'll probably find her in the rocking chair." This time I grinned. We had previously talked about moving and changing positions during labor to help things progress, but the subject of rocking chairs had never been mentioned.

When I entered the room Tonisha was pacing near the bed, reaching her arm around to rub her own lower back. Her mother was rocking in the chair, and two girlfriends lounged on the couch watching television. Marcus reclined on top of her bed. He hadn't been to any prenatal visits, but Tonisha told me he stayed with her throughout the pregnancy. I offered my hand, "Hi, you must be Marcus. I'm Veronica, Tonisha's midwife," and then quickly introduced myself to the rest of the group.

I watched quietly as Tonisha worked with a contraction. Bent over the bed, she grabbed Marcus' shirt and breathed rhythmically: "Aah. Ooh. Aah. Ooh. Aah. Ooh."

20

I gently put my hand on her shoulder, "Tonisha, you're doing such a good job. Keep it up." She flashed a quick grin.

Marcus looked up at me. "Can't you give her nothin' for the pain? She's hurtin' real bad. I can't take watchin' her. She's sufferin'."

I explained, "Tonisha chose to not use any pain medication. And she's doing just fine. We need to support her on this." Then I added emphatically, "I only want to hear positive comments for her. Right now, she's doing a terrific job. If I hear any negative remarks about how she's dealing with the pain, I'll ask you to leave." Scanning the crowd, I added, "Ya'll get it?" They all nodded.

Tonisha didn't ask for pain medication. She was willing to do whatever I suggested, changing positions frequently as her labor progressed. I also coached her with varied breathing patterns and reminded her to relax during the short intervals between contractions. As the force of contractions increased to another level of intensity, her fatigue began to show. "I know you're getting tired and this is getting a lot harder," I murmured. "Do you want some medication just to take the edge off?" She opened her eyes and glared at me.

Just after sunrise, Tonisha was ready to push. In a record sixteen minutes, her baby was delivered. I settled the squalling, perfect newborn on her chest and clamped off the umbilical cord. An astonished Marcus made the cut with his shaking hands.

After completing the paperwork, I visited Tonisha on the maternity ward. She cradled her newborn daughter in her arms while the maternity nurse helped her find a comfortable position for breastfeeding. I cheered, "Tonisha, you did it! You had your baby before your due date and," I emphasized, "you didn't use any drugs. Congratulations! You should be very proud of yourself. You did it your way, every step of the way."

And one more time, Tonisha beamed back at me with her incredible grin.

21

All Shook Up

Laurie is a solo practitioner in a sparsely populated area of the Rockies where the radio station routinely plays Elvis songs.

Elvis was still King in my part of the Rockies. The local radio station couldn't play enough of his music for the area's fans. But my idol was Candy, a midwife at our local hospital where I was completing my clinical rotation for nursing school. Candy made such an impression on me that I planned to follow in her footsteps.

First on my list of goals was to graduate from the nursing program. Second, I would work as a labor and delivery nurse where Candy would be my mentor. Third on my list was attending Candy's alma mater to complete my midwifery education. Finally, just like Candy, my plan was to find a place to practice where I could make a difference in women's lives. I had it all figured out.

Three years later, with the first two steps completed, I confidently sent an application to my target university for graduate school. Several months passed before the mail arrived that would launch me into the third part of my plan. "Well, finally, my acceptance letter," I assured myself. I flipped on the radio; a marathon of Elvis songs was playing. I held the envelope up to the sunlight, trying to read the answer through the paper. A thread of doubt suddenly crept into my mind as another familiar Elvis tune played:

If you find your sweetheart in the arms of a friend, that's when your heartaches begin. When dreams of a lifetime must come to an end, that's when your heartaches begin.

I sat paralyzed at the kitchen table remembering my early college years. I was such a typical freshman. Partying, having a good time, and making new friends were high on my agenda most every Friday and Saturday night. Sleeping until noon on Sunday to relieve the hangovers didn't help much. My grades took a big hit.

Staring at the unopened envelope, I tried to dismiss the fears that suddenly haunted me. My career goals had become more focused since meeting Candy. My grades had improved steadily and my references were very complimentary. Why shouldn't I be accepted?

As Elvis sang *I'm All Shook Up*, my hands trembled as I tore open the envelope and read, "We are sorry to inform you..."

Devastation hit. I sank into a chair and read the letter again. My GPA was one-tenth of a point below their requirements. I didn't make the cut off. Tears made their way down my face. How could this have happened? My plan to follow in Candy's footsteps had just been shattered. What would I do? Where would I go? To top it off, Elvis began singing *Return to Sender*. I turned off the radio.

Memories brought me back to the first time I heard about Candy. It was my junior year of nursing school and the beginning of our maternity rotation. Kathy, my nursing instructor, could only say good things about this midwife who welcomed students to observe her births. "Candy is a real trailblazer. You'll see what I mean when you meet her, Laurie," Kathy explained. Despite Kathy's positive description, I was unprepared for the impact Candy would have on my life.

My reverie then took me to the morning I arrived on the Labor and Delivery unit, anxious for my first day of clinical work and ready to put into practice what had been taught in class. Kathy informed me that Candy was working with a laboring woman, Ellie, who agreed to let me watch her birth. My eyes lit up and I practically squealed with delight.

So, eager to learn, I barged into the birthing room and stumbled against the table. Candy greeted me with a furrowed brow and her finger pressed up against her lip. What a great first impression I had made. Taking several steps backward into the corner, I watched with fascination. The lights were dimmed and curtains closed. Ellie's husband, Tom, laid a cool cloth on her forehead. Soft music murmured in the background while the ever-present Elvis serenaded:

Love me tender, love me true, all my dreams fulfilled.

23

For my darlin' I love you, and I always will.

Ellie was in the middle of a contraction. Her eyes were closed as she focused on slow rhythmic breathing. Tom was at her side counting softly in her ear as he gently held her hand. Candy sat at the foot of the bed, massaging her feet.

"Great job, Ellie. Keep up the good work. I know you can do this. Remember to take one contraction at a time," Candy encouraged. At the end of the contraction she listened to the baby's heart beat, then beckoned me over to the bedside and officially introduced me to Ellie and Tom.

Candy spoke quietly as she continued to massage Ellie's feet. "Laurie, your job today is to observe and learn. I'd like you to take notes on how I use all my senses to care for Ellie. Later we'll talk about some of the skills that create an outstanding labor and delivery nurse." I nodded my head in agreement and moved out of the laboring space.

For the next five hours I watched in amazement as Candy focused on Ellie and Tom. When Ellie asked for pain medication, Candy presented her with the various pharmacological options. There was a fast acting narcotic that could give her a break but also had the potential to depress the baby's respiration at birth. Then there was the big gun, the epidural, which would require an IV and confinement to bed, sometimes stalling labor progress.

Candy also offered several non-pharmacological alternatives. "Water can be magical in helping you through labor. You can stand or sit in the shower and use gravity to help move the baby's head down. We can direct the warm water on your back which feels good and relieves a lot of pressure. And there's also a bathtub for you to try." She added with a smile, "I have to tell you though, usually when I get patients in the bath or shower, they don't want to come out!"

Candy paused briefly and then continued, "At some point, it may be good for you to walk, sit on the birthing ball, or try the rocking chair. One of my favorite positions is to have you lean over the bed and rock your hips side to side. It really helps to move things along. Tom and I can take turns rubbing your back from that position too."

24

Then, taking me with her, Candy left the room to give the couple an opportunity to talk about their decision in private.

Tom found us a few minutes later, "Ellie would like to try the warm bath." His eyes glowed with pride that his Ellie had chosen a non-medical option.

I continued to watch. Candy verbally supported both partners as Ellie, with eyes closed, took breaths slowly and rhythmically in the tub of water.

Within an hour, Ellie's breathing changed dramatically. She suddenly exclaimed, "I have to push!" Candy directed Ellie to push through two contractions in the water before helping her dry off and return to the bed.

Ellie lay on her left side with Tom holding her upper leg. The nurse entered quietly and prepared for the birth. Low lighting, soft music, plus Candy's encouraging words and clear instructions accompanied David Edward's entry into the world. Afterwards I wrote furiously, eager to remember all that I seen.

Candy completed her paperwork, checked once more on Ellie, Tom and David, and then turned her attention to me. "Well, what did you learn today about using your senses?" Candy inquired.

My words poured out. "Candy, you were so in tune with that couple. You watched, touched, and listened. When you saw tension in Ellie's muscles, you gently touched the area that was tense and coached her to release it. You provided her with options that would both offer comfort and make sure labor progressed. You alerted the nurses for assistance when Ellie started pushing. There's so much more, and I still have lots of questions." I paused for a breath.

Candy laughed. "I might not have all the answers, but questions are always good. And don't you forget: Life is for learning. If you're alive, you should be eager to take in new knowledge. And asking questions is a part of the process. Now, let's hear the first question," she encouraged.

"Okay," I started. "What led you to become a midwife?"

"Good start," she responded. "I sometimes ask myself that same question, especially when I get tired or am up against a roadblock. There are many reasons I chose the profession of midwifery for my career." Candy took in a deep breath, pointed her index finger at me and began. "Number one, I like caring for people who are young and healthy. Women having babies fit these two categories."

She raised another finger. "Second, women are teachable yet vulnerable during times of change. What better way to use nursing skills, especially listening skills, to give encouragement and support to women during this incredible transition. Never forget, Laurie, listening to women is basic to midwifery."

As I took notes, her ring finger joined the others in the count, and she continued. "Third, women should have choices when they are having a baby, but they need a thorough explanation of the pros and cons of their options."

"Now don't get me wrong," she warned. "Some doctors have the time to do that, but many don't. Some doctors tell their female patients, 'It's my way or the highway.' The one thing I tell women is that they can have a baby any way they want as long as nothing compromises the safety of either the mother or the baby. Healthy, informed choices give women power."

Candy's little finger was next and a deep breath introduced a fourth reason. "Women are our sisters, so to speak. If you have a sister, you'll understand what I mean. It's hard to describe. Sisters understand each other. We are intuitive. We know each other. We learn from each other." She hesitated thoughtfully and then continued. "There's a spiritual bond that connects us on an intimate level during the birth of a baby. Birth is a spiritual event as well as a physical one. It is an honor to be invited to be a part of such an awesome occasion. That's exciting! I love being a part of it!"

Her thumb popped up. "Another reason I became a midwife is that I wanted a career that would make a difference for women."

She finished, "Well, I probably have said enough for you to digest. Do you have any more questions?"

"Not right now, but I'm sure there will be more after I take this all in," I responded. "Oh wait, one more thing. What is something that you've done in your career that really stands out for you?"

Cindy grinned, "I'm so happy you asked that. A few years ago, I worked

26

with our nursing organization lobbying for new laws to regulate how midwives practice in this state. It was a lot of work and took several years, but we persisted and got the job done!"

Still sitting in my cozy chair with the rejection letter in hand, I turned the radio back on. *Heartbreak Hotel* jolted me back to the present. Wondering what my idol Candy would think of my foiled plan, I read the letter again, still stunned.

I called a friend who graciously listened and allowed me to cry again. She reassured me, "In time, Laurie, a new plan will emerge. You are being pushed in a little different direction. Give yourself some time and space. It will become evident what your next step should be."

Following my wise friend's advice, I continued working at the hospital until a new plan emerged. I moved to another state, got hired as a Labor and Delivery nurse, and applied to a different graduate school. *It's Now or Never* became my theme song.

This time I waited more anxiously for a response, no longer so sure how my plan might turn out. When the letter arrived, I sat down to read it, braced for another rejection. Cautiously I opened the envelope, unfolded the letter, and then closed my eyes. Was I ready to see this? As I reluctantly squinted through my eyelashes, the words jumped out at me, "We are happy to inform you…"

Ecstatic, I called my long time friend and we celebrated over the phone.

Pouring myself into graduate school education, I was determined to be an A student, just like Candy. A requirement of our final semester included choosing a midwifery integration site. This provided an opportunity to hone in on my skills and put into practice all of my new knowledge. My first call was to Candy, who enthusiastically agreed to have me do this student experience with her as my mentor. I was thrilled!

So, after all this time, I spent my last semester with my idol. Elvis's words played in my head:

Please forget my past. The future's bright ahead.
Don't be cruel to a heart that's true.

27

As I blazed my trail, Candy was the idol who guided my way. To this day, I've remained her biggest fan, with Elvis coming in a very close second.

Respect My Elders

Michelle is a seasoned midwife in Minnesota where a large population of Hmong immigrants from Southeast Asia reside. In the Hmong culture, the elders are often called upon to make decisions during tough family situations.

"My mother says she will wait for the elders to come. Then the decision will be made," Lo's eldest daughter Kia informed me, interpreting for her mother.

It was midnight. Lo was a forty-two year-old Hmong woman in early labor with her eighth baby. I placed my hands once again on her pendulous belly, muscles overstretched from previous pregnancies. The baby's head remained at the top of her abdomen in a breech position. Lo's contractions remained mild and far apart. "Thank goodness," I thought, "These light contractions give us time to evaluate this baby's position and whether or not we can do a vaginal delivery."

Her face was expressionless, just like the other Hmong women I have attended in labor. These stoic women often showed no emotion, even up to the moment before they gave birth.

The obstetricians looked at Lo's pelvic x-ray and determined the safest way to deliver her baby would be by cesarean. Western medicine and technology is rarely questioned in such a clear-cut case, but for this Hmong family the questions were just beginning. For them surgery brings a greater risk than bleeding or infection. The incision involved with this procedure posed a significant spiritual risk to the mother.

The Hmong believe there are good and evil spirits in the world. They believe that when the body is vulnerable, such as during surgery, it can be invaded by these ominous entities. Furthermore, the body can also be invaded by the ghost spirits left behind by those who have died in the hospital. This is the risk that Lo, her family, and her elders feared the most from a cesarean birth.

The baby, according to the Hmong beliefs, does not acquire its spirit until three days after its birth. It is very important for the baby to be at home when this happens. Thus, Hmong mothers will do everything possible to be home by the third day after delivery, cesarean birth or not.

As a midwife, I would normally transfer a woman with a breech baby to the physicians who would then take care of the situation, but I couldn't do that with Lo. She saw a midwife consistently throughout this pregnancy and expected a midwife to discuss this new dilemma with her and her family.

And discuss we did. Her husband, son, and daughter remained in the labor room. Although they wanted to wait for the elders to arrive, it was important to me that they understand the situation at that moment–a situation that could quickly turn into an emergency should Lo's contractions get stronger and more frequent.

I described in detail the risk to the baby if Lo attempted a vaginal birth. "The head is hyper-extended, looking up to the sky, like this." I raised my head up to the ceiling. "This position makes it much harder for the baby to come out. The legs are pointed upwards and crossed at the knees. Once the lower body comes out, the head can get caught by the cervix."

For the family to fully understand the risk to this baby, it would be necessary for me be very graphic with my explanation. I placed my hands under my chin and encircled my fingers around my neck. "The head can get stuck in this way." Kia interpreted my words for her mother and father, with little pause between her phrases.

They discussed the situation in Hmong with each other. I patiently waited, listening to the unique cadences of their language. At times they seemed to be all talking at once. Then they would periodically pause and look to the father. They conversed some more. I remained grateful Lo was not having strong contractions yet, or there would be no time for these lengthy explanations.

Again Kia told me, "We will wait for the elders to come before deciding." Instead of using a western focus on individuality, the Hmong worked as a group. These Hmong leaders had the authority to make the final decision in complicated cases such as this.

"When will that be?" I asked nervously.

"In the morning," she replied.

30

I caught my breath. There was a good chance this baby would try to be born before then. Anticipating that it could be another eight or nine hours before they would get to the hospital, I questioned, "How early do they get up?"

"Four in the morning," she answered, and then clarified, "They will be here by 4:00 A.M."

Looking at my watch I calculated, "Four hours. That's not as late as it could be."

"All right," I responded. "We'll try to wait until then."

I walked out of the room and said a prayer that labor would stay quiet and active contractions would hold off. The midwife in me didn't want to wait a minute longer to prepare for a cesarean delivery, but under these unique circumstances, I honored the wishes of Lo and her family.

"I'll be in the call room resting until the elders come," I told the nurse. "But please wake me if you see her contractions getting any stronger or closer, okay?" She nodded in agreement. I gave the consulting physician a call and updated him on the situation. Fortunately, he understood the Hmong culture. He agreed to hold off on doing the cesarean until the relatives arrived and we could obtain Lo's consent for the surgery.

I put my head on the pillow, astonished to find I could wait this one out. Normally, we'd all be heading to the operating room right now.

The phone woke me at 4:00 A.M. *"They're all here,"* the nurse told me. The tone of her voice implied we were going to have a room full. I hopped out of bed, washed my face, and headed back to labor and delivery.

The room was packed with at least twenty elders, plus Lo and her family. Murmurs of Hmong chatter floated from one to another. Most were men, but I noticed a few older women there as well. I asked Kia if she would continue to interpret for her family. She discussed this in Hmong with her family, and then responded in English, "Yes, I will."

Speaking one sentence at a time I introduced myself and paused, giving Kia time to share my words with the group. It became quiet as they listened closely. The situation and risk to the baby was explained in detail. Holding up the x-ray in

31

the light for all to see, I pointed to the baby's head and again emphasized the dangerous position. These significant concerns were reviewed three more times.

Standing quietly, I waited. Now it was up to them. The chatter began again and seemed to crescendo. The twenty elders talked in gatherings of three or four, then shared their thoughts openly with the whole group. They appeared to be looking at every angle of this unusual and challenging situation. While considering the technology of our Western world where they now lived, they also held onto the spiritual beliefs held by their culture for centuries.

Forty-five minutes elapsed. Then more pauses occurred, a change from the nonstop sentences that began these conversations. Not wanting to interfere with their process, I remained silent and waited a bit longer.

Then there was a major pause. I quietly whispered to Kia, "Do they have any more questions for me?"

She interpreted my inquiry, focusing on a man who appeared to be the leader. He talked to the people around him, then back to Kia. "He wants to see the x-ray again." I tried to read his thoughts. "What does this mean?" I wondered. I held the x-ray up to the light and summarized the dangers one more time.

He addressed the family members who listened attentively. He paused when a few responded in their native language. Looking at the fetal monitor and seeing more contractions, I thought, "It's time for a decision."

Kia and the head elder conferred once more before including Lo and her husband in the discussion. Finally, Kia looked to me and said, "We will do the cesarean."

It was 5:30 A.M. I called the physician and nurses who promptly notified the operating room and prepared for surgery. The relatives slowly left the room. A few remained in the lobby to await the results of the birth. Kia continued to interpret. I explained to Lo what procedures would be done to prepare her for the cesarean. She maintained a stoic expression on her face as we wheeled her down to the operating room.

The surgical team was ready. Within ten minutes, they delivered a robust baby boy. With his first breath, he let out a wondrous wail. The surgeon handed him over to the newborn team. His legs remained perched upward just as they had been positioned in the womb. The nurses wrapped him snugly in warmed blankets.

I walked out to the waiting room and pulled the mask from my face. "All is well," I told Lo's family and remaining elders. "Lo has given birth to a son! Congratulations!" They smiled and nodded to one another. They had made a decision to use Western technology. But they did it their way, the Hmong way.

You Have To Tell Me!

Just beginning her career as a nurse-midwife, Josie learns to respond to a patient who places a high premium on control.

Without first telling her, the anesthesia crew quickly laid Carrie down onto the operating table. She demanded, "Come on, you guys! You have to tell me what's going on! Give me a little heads up here. I *need* to know." Carrie had just received a spinal injection for her cesarean birth. Not all patients are this outspoken, much less in the operating room; however Carrie insisted that she know ahead of time what was going to happen to her right down to the tiniest detail.

As we waited for surgery to begin, I remembered a midwife mentor who once advised me, "Josie, try to anticipate what might occur with your patients. Tell them the possibilities ahead of time so that if something does happen, it won't be such a shock." I learned early in Carrie's pregnancy not only to anticipate but to "hyper-anticipate" all the possible outcomes. It became very apparent that for Carrie it would be emotionally disastrous to have anything unexpected come her way.

As a midwife, I tried to analyze why women like Carrie developed this exceptionally strong need to be in control. My midwife research led me to understand it could come from some unexpected shock or trauma that occurred in childhood, something totally out of their control. It could be the trauma of parents divorcing or an incident of abuse, including sexual molestation. Although Carrie never wanted to share any details of her past, I suspected she had experienced some type of unpredictable trauma as a young child.

Carrie first came to me wearing a Columbia fleece jacket, camouflage pants, and hiking boots. Her short hair fit her active outdoor lifestyle. Our discussions revealed a fierce passion for the environment and an unshakable commitment to feminism. At age thirty-four and highly educated, Carrie and her husband, Nick, were expecting their first baby.

34

During each prenatal visit, she opened her day planner to a myriad list of questions. Already at eight weeks along, Carrie asked very specific questions about labor and delivery. "Josie, will I be able to sit in a bathtub when I'm having contractions? What can I eat and drink during labor? Will I be allowed to walk? How often do you check my cervix for progress? How often do you do episiotomies? Can I choose my own labor and delivery nurse if I don't like the one who's assigned to me?"

Prepping in the operating room for Carrie's cesarean, Nick sat on the stool next to Carrie, holding her hand. He lightly kissed her forehead. The staff unfolded the drapes over Carrie's body leaving her belly exposed and ready for surgery.

I reflected on the chain of events during this long labor as the operating team completed their checklist. Carrie had walked through most of her earlier contractions. When they got stronger she stood in a steamy shower which soothed her aching body. When the cervix did not dilate past 5 cm, the bag of water was broken. Later, with no progress and after much convincing, Pitocin was started to strengthen the contractions. Despite all of our best efforts, progress did not come. Pictures from home, soothing background music, and multiple position changes did not lead to a vaginal delivery.

It had been a long day and night. My body ached with even the slightest movement and I craved sleep. It had been an endless, exhausting process in which I hyper-anticipated for Carrie each step of the way. My brain could hardly take in any more information or make one more decision. I was hitting the wall.

Still analyzing Carrie's labor, I helped the nursing staff open instrument packs. During active labor, I had forewarned Carrie, "Sometimes we need to put in an internal monitor to better see how the baby is responding to contractions. We don't need to do it right now, but I want to give you a chance to think about it and ask any questions you might have. This procedure may need to be done quickly if the baby's heart beat shows signs of distress."

35

This was followed by more explanations. "Even though you're having strong contractions and trying all sorts of positions, the baby's head is still high in the pelvis. It's not moving down as it should be. And the cervix is not dilating."

And finally, the recommendation came. "It's been more than two hours of strong contractions with no progress. Carrie and Nick, we'll need to do a cesarean birth to deliver your baby. I've consulted with my physician about this and she agrees." I again hyper-anticipated and reviewed the operating room procedures, the potential complications, and the possible outcomes of this major surgery. "I'll give you some time alone to talk about it." Since the baby's heart beat was stable, Nick and Carrie chose to keep trying.

Within the next fifteen minutes the baby's heart beat was showing the beginning signs of stress. The physician and I explained our concerns to them, "We absolutely recommend a cesarean birth to safely deliver your baby." In the end, they agreed to have the surgery.

"Josie, what's happening?" Carrie asked from behind the blue drapes, jolting me back to the reality of the operating room. As the anesthesiologist hung a new intravenous bag, she continued, "Have they started yet?"

"They are testing the spinal anesthetic to make sure you're numb, and it looks like you are. Now they're starting the first incision." Still hyper-anticipating, I further explained, "Okay Carrie—it's time to get ready. You're going to feel a very bizarre sensation in your abdomen as they deliver your baby. It shouldn't hurt and it only lasts a few seconds. I'll tell you when we're close." The very last of my adrenaline kicked in for the birth.

"Where are they now? What are they doing?" Carrie continued to ask.

"It sure would be nice if she could let go for just a few moments, now that we're in the midst of surgery," I wished to myself. But Carrie's constant questions confirmed her need to maintain control at all times. I looked up and caught the eye of the surgeon glancing over her mask, first towards Carrie and then to me. Her eyebrows raised in response to Carrie's endless questions. I nodded understandingly and continued to answer them.

"Okay, Carrie," I warned, "Get ready to feel that weird sensation I told you about. We are just about to celebrate your baby's birthday!"

Her eyes widened. "I feel it!" she said ecstatically, and then "Whoa!" This was quickly followed by a huge sigh from Carrie as her baby was lifted up, filling the room with its sweet, newborn voice.

The next day I trudged slowly up the stairway to Carrie's room. My muscles were still tired and sore from the long shift the day before. My legs felt like lead. I used the handrail to give me a boost. With each heavy step, my mind tried to focus on what to anticipate for Carrie during this postpartum visit.

I tapped softly on the door, not wanting to wake a sleeping baby, and heard, "Come in." Carrie's baby was snuggled on her chest, sound asleep. Mother and daughter looked very content.

"Hello! How are you doing?" I asked in a whisper. "And how are you feeling about everything that happened?"

Carrie grinned. "Oh, Josie, I'm doing wonderful. I got great care. You midwives are great! Thank you for everything!"

I nodded in appreciation and relief. Before totally relaxing, I caught my breath thinking, "It's time to hyper-anticipate cesarean recovery and new motherhood for Carrie." Predictably, she grabbed her long list of questions from the bedside table. I held back a sigh, biting my lip. After reviewing her post-surgical instructions we started at the top of her list and chatted for over an hour. Then, I tried my best to give her a little heads-up on the next eighteen years of childrearing.

Chapter 2: Life Choices

How we make choices in our life is an individual process, as unique as our fingertips, and guided by our priorities. Whether expected or unexpected, everyday or monumental, our choices have lasting, rippling effects.

A Foot in Both Worlds

Anne joins a large metropolitan midwifery practice which serves women from a variety of cultures and age groups. One of her first patients is Debra, a Hmong teenager, who shares her world with Anne. As Anne is reassigned to different clinics over the next few years, Debra follows.

As a fifteen-year-old Hmong girl, Debra had a foot in both worlds. I met her during one of my first days practicing as a midwife at a high school clinic. Typical of other teenagers, she wore a tee shirt emblazoned with an American rock band logo. Yet Debra's shy smile and sweet voice were characteristic of her Hmong heritage. Similarly, Debra was very petite, and on that particular day, she was also twelve-weeks pregnant.

I was just beginning to learn about the Hmong, many of whom were now settled in this country. Their history spanned thousands of years in Southeast Asia, after migrating from China to Laos. Debra's ancestors played a vital role during the Viet Nam war, sacrificing their lives to assist the United States. I remembered those tumultuous times during my own teenage years, before Debra was even born. But on that particular clinic day, the ripples of war continued for us both.

"Debra," I gently asked, "What brought you to the United States?"

Her reticence melted as she began her story. "Anne, I came here with my aunt, uncle, and cousins from Laos when I was about four years old. We escaped out of our country to live in the refugee camps in Thailand. After a couple years, we moved to California where other relatives were living."

"Where were your parents?" I asked.

"They were killed." She paused, and then continued, "My parents had gold coins hidden in their pockets. They saved up this money to get out of Laos. The killers must have known. I was tiny and hid behind a tree. It was dark. No one knew I was there. They were all in the woods. I saw the robbers shoot my parents in the head and heard their bodies fall to the ground. The murderers went

40

through their clothes, grabbed the coins, and ran away." Debra's voice remained calm as she described this horrific crime.

"Oh, Debra, that must have been a nightmare for you," I responded. It was impossible to comprehend what it must have been like for Debra to witness the murder of her own parents, much less at such a young age.

"Even though I was so young," she explained, "I remember it very clearly. But Anne, what happened to me in California still confuses me."

"Tell me more," I encouraged.

"I lived there with my relatives in a house next to a cemetery. There was a huge car accident in our town. A newly married couple were killed in the crash and they were buried in that cemetery. I was only six years old but went to that cemetery every day and visited their graves and cried and cried. I didn't even know them. Why do you think I did that? Do you think it was because I missed my own parents?" Her questions hung in the air as we pondered the answers.

Then I quietly responded, "Yeah. I sure think so."

Debra dutifully returned to the high school clinic for every prenatal visit. She had a traditional Hmong marriage, but also a very American lifestyle. Debra wore blue jeans and t-shirts, along with a threaded Hmong bracelet to ward off evil spirits. During one visit, I asked Debra to write down everything she ate over the next three days. When she gave me the list, it included french fries from the school cafeteria for lunch and rice, chicken, and vegetables for her supper at home.

A few months later, Debra gave birth to a healthy son. When she returned to the high school clinic, I asked about her plans for birth control. In my past experiences, the older Hmong women I'd delivered often responded, "I will talk with my husband about it," which translated into "No, thank you." But because Debra seemed more adapted to American culture, I expected her to have a more modern response.

To my surprise, Debra answered, "I will talk with my grandmother about that." She quickly changed the subject and described how her meals consisted of chicken, rice, and water for the whole month following her birth, a common Hmong tradition. "Anne, I am *so tired* of chicken, I can't wait to have some

41

pizza!" she complained with her ever-present smile. Although in many ways she was very much an American teen, she respectfully followed the traditions of her family origins too. And that tradition included a refusal of birth control.

A couple years later I was reassigned to a downtown women's clinic. Debra followed me there and saw me for her second pregnancy. She had just graduated from high school.

When I was moved yet again to a suburban clinic, Debra was on my schedule for her third pregnancy. I was touched and honored that she kept coming to me for care.

Following her third birth, I asked, "Debra, do you have any desire for birth control at this time?" I expected the same response she gave after her first baby was born.

But Debra answered differently this time. "Yes. I have three kids. I'm taking college classes. My husband helps out a lot, but our family keeps us very busy. I don't want any more children right now." We discussed the various birth control options available. She chose a birth control injection to prevent a future pregnancy.

Debra continued to see me every year for her annual exams and birth control follow-up. Each time, she shared more about her life. Unlike traditional Hmong women who stay at home to care for their large families, Debra continued her education. She explained, "My husband and I realized that we have a choice – to follow the traditional Hmong way of life or to live like Americans. We have chosen the American way. He supports my goals and wants me to get a college degree." Yet, just as with other Hmong families, Debra's mother-in-law lived with their family and provided childcare.

This became especially vital when Debra graduated from college and enrolled in a six-month internship, two hours away from home. "Your husband must be very supportive," I commented.

"Oh, he is," she acknowledged. "But it is hard. I miss him and my kids so much when I am gone. But it is what I need to do. And my mother-in-law takes good care of the family when I'm gone."

42

A couple months later, I opened the newspaper and was surprised to see Debra's photo on the front page. She earned an award for her educational achievements and had been chosen to be a member of a special state task force. My heart swelled with pride for her.

Ten years after my first visit with Debra, I had my final clinic day with this midwifery practice. It was very emotional for me to see many of my long-term patients for the last time.

"You have an add-on visit at the end of the afternoon," my nurse informed me. Grabbing the last chart, I walked into the room and saw Debra. "Oh, my goodness! It's wonderful to see you! You were one of my very first patients when I joined this midwife team ten years ago. It's so fitting that you're here today. Tell me what's been happening in your life." We talked on and on. My mind flashed back to all the visits we had together. I gently asked, "Do you remember telling me about your parents and about the cemetery you visited as a little girl?" She nodded, recounting the story in every detail once again. It was an everlasting part of her history.

"Debra, from the little girl hiding behind the tree to the extraordinary young woman you are today, you've worked hard and accomplished so much. You must feel so very proud and satisfied." She smiled. We considered the sequence of events that had brought her halfway around the world to where she was that day. Debra had a foot in both worlds, and she had taken the best of each to create her own unique path.

Quiet Power

Fifty-two years old and a newly graduated midwife, Rayleen leaves Northern Michigan to work at a birth center on the Texas-Mexico border. In this humble setting, Rayleen experiences a rich Hispanic tradition through one woman's quiet power.

In Hispanic tradition, men do not attend the births of their children. I know this now. As a new midwife, however, I was oblivious to the rich culture and subtle nuances of San Perlita.

During those first warm Rio Grande evenings, I felt far away from my home in Northern Michigan. Having just graduated from my midwifery program, I had accepted a five-month fellowship at a birth center in San Perlita, a rural town near the Mexican border. The birth center cared for many migrant workers who labored in the dusty Texan heat. They lived in a *colonia,* an impoverished neighborhood of cement-block shacks.

Lola was one of my first patients at the San Perlita birth center. Like many migrant workers, Lola came for prenatal care very late in her pregnancy. She visited inconsistently, coming only two or three times before her delivery. In a different setting, care providers might have considered Lola noncompliant or irresponsible. But I saw Lola differently. Determination and strength shimmered in her dark brown eyes. Already the mother of six girls, Lola lived a life of struggle, but she knew how to work hard, and childbirth was no exception.

When Lola went into labor, I instructed her husband Juan to stay with her at the birth center overnight, revealing my cultural ignorance. Too polite to disagree, Juan did as I asked. Sitting beside Lola in a rocking chair, I placed my hand at the top of her uterus. Throughout the evening her contractions remained mild and far apart. Although she was fluent in both English and Spanish, Lola was speechless that night. Hard work does not require any words. She sat in the double bed with Juan at her side. I quietly watched for the cues of progressing labor–deep breathing, sweat above the lips, eyes shut firmly.

44

I did not talk, cheer, or instruct Lola as she breathed through her contractions, but instead let her find her own way. My job was to give Lola a calm environment to concentrate and find her own inner strength. Too many times laboring women are distracted by a rush of activity and overzealous instructions. Labor and delivery staff can be so busy that they don't take time to watch and wait. They end up missing the woman's cues. To me, that's not good care. That's not midwifery.

Sitting contentedly, I observed and waited in this peaceful birth center. With her contractions still infrequent, Lola and Juan fell asleep. I covered them with a blanket and turned out the lights. The moonlight filtered down through the window above us. Silver shadows floated over the delivery cart and baby warmer in the corner. As I walked to the adjacent birthing room, my shoes tapped lightly across the linoleum floor. The sliding glass door was left open so I could hear when Lola's labor intensified. At that moment, the only sound was soft snoring.

While I was lying on the bed and still listening for any new noises, the words of my midwife instructor drifted back to me, "You know how the hospital staff will treat her. We will take good care of her." I shut my eyes remembering back to one specific day as a midwife student. No one else had wanted to take a 400-pound laboring woman as their patient. But my instructor had insisted that midwives accept the socially outcast patients and treat them with respect. As a migrant worker with little prenatal care, Lola fit this category of social outcast. I tried to consider how she might have been treated in a hospital setting and kept thinking, "Thank goodness she is here."

Before long, the early rays of sunrise replaced the cool moonlight shadows. Spanish murmurs filtered in from the room next door. Covers rustled as Juan got out of bed. I walked to the sink and splashed cool water on my face. Drying my face with a towel, I looked in the mirror and could see Juan's reflection. He was dressed and nodding his head as Lola talked. He kissed her forehead and walked out of the room. I came into Lola's room as Juan's car revved up in the parking log.

"Good morning, Lola, Did you get some good sleep?"

45

She looked up at me calmly and merely said, "Come." I looked closer and was stunned. Her face instantly turned serious and red. She began pushing. Without thinking I grabbed the delivery cart and put on my gloves. Within a minute, Lola had given birth to a baby boy.

I was awestruck. Then it hit me. "Aha!" I said to myself. The lesson of this past night was suddenly very clear to me. For Lola, men were not to be present during labor and birth, not even her husband. She had known just when to send him home. A cloud of dust from the gravel road still hung in the air.

I stood back, amazed, having just witnessed an intense power. *A quiet power.*

This Path Chose Me

Gerri is a student midwife with clearly set goals and high expectations for herself. She learns a valuable lesson of acceptance from her patient Katie in a Chicago maternity unit.

Katie's body said it all. Her eyes were glued to a focal point with her lips slightly parted and tongue lightly pressed against the back of her top teeth. Katie's forehead was wrinkle free. Her shoulders sagged away from her neck. Katie did steady rhythmic breathing in time with her husband's cadence.

They looked like the picture-perfect Lamaze-prepared couple. The increased pace of the rocking chair every four to five minutes indicated that Katie was having a contraction. My hand, gently placed at the top of Katie's uterus, confirmed what the accelerated rocking demonstrated.

Katie and Jarrod were determined to have a medication-free birth and a healthy baby. A sports duffle bag near Jarrod contained lip balm, hard candy, a tennis ball in a sock, lotion, back massager, a small fan, and several other tools needed to facilitate their success. I hadn't seen a couple so prepared in a long time. They appeared ready for any challenges that might come their way.

The labor journey for Katie began at one o'clock that morning. Following her third trip to the bathroom, Katie whispered, "Jarrod, I'm in labor."

"What? How do you know?" he questioned sleepily.

Katie had wrapped a small throw around her shoulders. "I noticed some bloody mucus like they said in class. And I'm feeling pain above my pubic bone about every five minutes."

Jarrod bolted upright in bed. "Well, don't you think we should call the midwife?"

Katie placed her hand on Jarrod's shoulder and pushed gently, "No, not yet. It's still mild. Go back to sleep. I'll wake you when I need you to help me deal with the pain. I just wanted you to know."

47

Eight hours later in the hospital birthing room, both Katie and Jarrod perspired as they worked together to stay in control. They were excited to learn that the cervix was dilated to four centimeters. My expectations were high for a lovely vaginal delivery with this perfect Lamaze couple. I thought, "This is going to be a beautiful birth. I just know it."

With each contraction, Jarrod heaped praise and encouragement upon Katie. "You are doing an awesome job, honey. Keep up the good work. Concentrate on your focal point. Here's a sip of water. Soon, the baby will be here, and our precious Sarah will be cradled in your arms."

By mid-afternoon, we were all anxious to discover if there had been any progress. After checking Katie's cervix, I was a little concerned that it remained at four centimeters. Options for enhancing labor progress were reviewed with Katie and Jarrod. "We could continue to change your position. You could get up and do some walking. Or we could start a Pitocin drip to improve the frequency and strength of the contractions. Another way to speed things up is to break your bag of waters and see what happens. We could try that before starting the Pitocin."

Katie and Jarrod chose to have the waters broken and then sit in the rocking chair. We would re-examine Katie in two hours.

I rationalized to myself, "This is just a little bump in the road that couples often experience during their first labor."

Two hours later, dinnertime brought a further inquiry about Katie's progress. With Katie's consent, I examined her again. The cervix remained unchanged. "I think it's time to start an IV, place the internal fetal monitor, and begin some Pitocin before you get too tired and don't have enough energy to push."

Both agreed to the interventions. I continued to be amazed at their flexibility and adaptability.

The nurse efficiently placed the monitors on Katie. She brought in the IV bag mixed with Pitocin. "This has *got* to work for them," I told myself.

Eighteen hours from the start of labor, Katie and Jarrod persisted in their efforts. They used all the tricks and tools they learned in class. The duffle bag sat empty. Lying on her left side with a pillow between her knees, Katie remained relaxed and focused.

Jarrod was faithful with his verbal support during each contraction. Her cleansing breath signaled a new contraction. He instructed Katie, "In, two, three. Out, two, three. In, two, three. Out, two, three." His calm voice provided clear instruction. At the end of the contraction Jared praised Katie, "You are awesome, honey. Our daughter will be so proud of her mom, just like I am." He planted another kiss on her forehead. With the contraction over, Jarrod gently pressed on Katie's shoulder to check for any tension. "Keep up the good work. I know you're getting tired. Your labor will be over soon."

"This couple doesn't let anything get in the way of their positive attitude, even when things haven't been going their way," I noted to myself. Their endurance and patience was impressive. It had to pay off.

When we checked the cervix again several hours later, it had not budged. Discouraged, I shook my head and reported, "I was so hopeful that there would be some change, but you're still at four centimeters. The monitor shows you're having strong, frequent contractions. I'm so sorry this is happening. We've done everything possible to make progress. It's time to consult the obstetrician." Katie and Jarrod nodded.

Dr. Telmar examined Katie. "I agree with the midwife's assessment. You can continue to labor for a couple more hours, but with all that you have already tried, I recommend a cesarean section. Would you like some time to think about it?" Katie and Jarrod simultaneously shook their heads no.

Dr. Telmar reviewed the risks of the surgery, and Katie signed the consent form. As the nurses prepped Katie, I stood there feeling completely disappointed. Having a cesarean was the right thing to do, but I remained baffled by this outcome. It simply should not have happened. We all did everything right.

I shared with Katie, "I'm totally frustrated by what's happened. And I'm sorry. Maybe I should have..."

Katie's brow suddenly furrowed as she held up her hand, stopping me mid-sentence. She placed her hand on mine; her eyes relaxed. "Gerri, please

49

don't go through all the possible 'maybes' and 'what-if's.' It's not helpful for me. I learned a long time ago that I don't always get everything in life that I want. What's important is to experience each situation at hand. Jarrod and I have done what we could do, and we're confident we've done our best. We have not failed. And you have not failed. We all just needed to take another path—different from the one we originally planned." She paused and smiled at me. "You know, sometimes the path chooses us."

Just then the nurses moved her onto a stretcher and rolled Katie to the operating suite with Jarrod. This was the different path. After scrubbing in, I joined the surgical team. We all cheered as their beautiful baby entered the world.

As I took my usual route home that evening, Katie's philosophical message echoed in my mind. Sometimes life, including labor and birth, takes us down a very different road from what we imagined and planned for. It's not necessarily bad—just different.

Later that week I came upon a country road that for years had begged me to take the longer, more scenic way home. I made a sudden left turn onto this bumpy, tree-lined country lane. It must have been Katie's philosophy making its way into my life. Sometimes the path chooses us.

Mother Influences

Gina catches her Mother's passion for birth, beginning in the South African bush.

"Can you believe someone's going to give me a master's degree?" I asked my friend Darla.

"And worse yet," she teased, "they're going to let you be a midwife!"

Suddenly it hit me, "I'm really going to be a midwife." I put on my robe for the graduation ceremony and remembered defending my career choice to many people–people who thought I should go into business or medicine. But they didn't understand the love of midwifery that had been growing inside me since I was a child.

I was six years old the day my mom returned home from the South African bush. She was unable to stop talking about the tribal midwives she had just met. As a Lamaze instructor, she had gone out to the country to share her obstetric knowledge with them. But it was clearly my mom who was inspired by the midwives. As she told her stories, I remember thinking, *"She wants to be one of them."* As a young child I wasn't sure exactly what that meant, but it didn't surprise me when she applied to the midwifery program in Johannesburg, four hours away.

After completing her education our family returned to the U.S. As we settled back into the American way of life, Mom began interviewing for a midwifery position, but jobs were scarce at the time. Following an interview at a birth center, she declared it was the only place she ever wanted to work.

That same week we were invited to a friend's house for a barbecue. While the steaks sizzled on the grill, Mom checked her phone messages. Suddenly she was jumping up and down, with tears streaming down her reddened cheeks. "I got it! I got the job!" she yelled at the top of her voice. Mom had her first official midwife job at the birth center.

My mom loved being a midwife. One particular Saturday morning about 6 A.M., I heard her car door slam in our driveway and realized that she had been out all night at a birth. I threw on my robe and went down to the kitchen. The dark circles under her eyes told of her fatigue.

I sat across the table from her. Placing her hands around a fresh cup of coffee, Mom described from beginning to end all that happened during the woman's labor and delivery, the joys along with the challenges. As she talked, Mom radiated a passionate energy. I realized then how much she loved bringing babies into the world and how fulfilling this work was to her. I asked, "Can I go with you to see a birth?"

"Let's see, you're twelve years old now," she pondered. "I think that'd be great."

A couple weeks later, Mom called to me, "Gina, here's your chance to see a birth. Beth is in labor and said its okay for you come watch her delivery. We have to hurry, though. It's her fifth baby." We hopped in the car and headed for the birth center.

The events surrounding this birth have been etched in my memory forever. Beth was already waiting for us in the parking lot when we arrived. She stopped on the steps of the birth center to breathe through a contraction as Mom unlocked the door. Her husband and kids waited in the lobby while we climbed the stairs to one of the birthing rooms.

Mom checked her cervix as I stood against the wall, not wanting to be in the way. Beth was fully dilated and ready to deliver. Mom picked up the phone and called the nurse to come quickly and then frantically opened the sterile equipment. Beth began to push the baby out. With three pushes the baby girl was born.

When the baby struggled with her first breath, Mom startled me, "Gina, go quickly down the hall to the closet on the left and bring the oxygen tank right away."

I raced down the hall and hurried back to the room with the tank. Mom placed the oxygen mask on the baby's face. After a few whiffs of oxygen, the baby began to cry and pinked up beautifully. She was just fine.

The crying brought her siblings scurrying up the stairs to see their new little sister. Mom whispered softly to me, "You did so well! You saved the baby."

Several years later, I attended another birth with my mother. Jane, who was having her third baby at home, specifically asked me to come to provide support for her mother and children. I played with the children in their yard while Mom worked with Jane. Her labor went very smoothly. When I checked in to see what was happening, there was Mom gently massaging Jane's back. Later she was sitting outside the shower stall offering encouragement, repeatedly saying, "Jane, you're doing such a good job. Keep up the good work."

Soon Mom called, "Gina, bring the kids and come to the master bedroom." With the delivery imminent, I stood off to the side holding the three-year old in my arms and clasping the hand of the six-year old. Their grandmother crouched behind me, grasping my shoulders, her face pressed into my back. Every once in awhile, she peeked over my shoulder and asked, "What's happening?" Then she would quickly press her head back into my shoulder blade. I provided moment-by-moment commentary for her and the children during each step of the birth.

As the dark wet hair appeared at the vaginal opening, I explained, "Oh look, there's the baby's head."

"Is it really?" the grandmother questioned. She took a quick look and then focused downward, pressing her forehead against my shoulder.

"Absolutely," I exclaimed. With one more push the head was born and the rest of the baby quickly followed. Hearing the newborn's lusty cry, everyone began crying. The grandma soaked the back of my blouse with her tears. Within a few minutes, the kids climbed onto the bed between their parents to touch and hold their new brother. I was deeply moved by the closeness of their family. It was also inspiring to see the role my mother had played in helping them to have such an intimate birth experience in their own home.

In fact, that event stayed with me as I got into high school and started thinking about a career. Nothing else sparked my interest like midwifery. I had found my passion and couldn't wait to tell my mom, "I've decided to follow in your footsteps."

I expected Mom to be absolutely thrilled with my career choice but instead, she appeared disinterested. I was shocked to hear her noncommittal response, "Oh, okay. Are you sure this is what you really want?"

One day I asked Mom to help me select a college and school of nursing to get my dream started. She had other things to do. I was totally perplexed by her attitude. Finally, I confronted her. "What is going on here? You're not being very supportive. Why?"

She started to cry. "I know, honey. Some of the midwives are concerned that I'm somehow forcing you to go into this profession. Gina, that is the last thing I want to do," she explained.

Frustrated, I yelled back at her, "Why do you care what they think? You know you never forced me. Look, I'm going to nursing school and then on to midwifery. Are you going to help me or not? This is what I want to do!"

After four years in the nursing program and two more years in the midwifery program, I placed the graduation hat on my head and found my place in the processional line. Walking down aisle with my head high, I passed my mother. A huge smile lit up her face and tears filled her eyes. Darla winked at me.

After receiving my diploma, I again spotted my mom in the audience. She beamed and signaled a thumbs up. I smiled widely back. There was no way to stifle my cheer, "I did it. I'm a midwife, just like my mom!"

Is There A Doctor In The House?

Marcie practices midwifery in the southern part of the United States where an old-fashioned view of a granny midwife skews a mother's perception.

"We want a doctor for my daughter," demanded Sophia's mother as I entered the birthing room. Her glare clearly meant, "And *not* a midwife." Her eyes locked on mine as she stood with her hands on her broad hips, blocking my view of Sophia. She was undeterred in her stance.

I knew Sophia very well having seen her for every prenatal visit. She was counting on me to attend her birth. I started to get angry and then saw Sophia's tear-stained face peeking around her mother. She was biting her lip, and her eyes pleaded, "Marcie, don't leave me." Tom, her husband, stood on the other side of the birthing bed. His arms were crossed and he seemed embarrassed by his mother-in-law as he shuffled from one foot to the other.

This would take some diplomacy. I chose my words very carefully while raising an eyebrow. "Why, I'd be happy to have Dr. Bates work with us today. He's a new family medicine resident on the obstetric service. I'll have him complete your admission physical exam, Sophia." I further explained that Dr. Bates would assist during the delivery. I smiled at Sophia with a wink and a nod, without saying the words, "Trust me."

When Dr. Bates entered the birthing room, I introduced him to the family. While I was standing at the foot of the bed observing him complete the exam, he looked at me and said, "I think we need to call Dr. Santos. She has a vaginal defect."

"Sophia, Tom, and I talked about this during their first prenatal visit," I responded. "It's a very minor septum—a thin bit of tissue in the vaginal area. It should resolve itself once Sophia begins to push. Dr. Santos is aware of the situation. Don't worry. We don't need to call him at this time." Sophia's mother listened intently as I further explained to the resident, "We might need to clip the septum at the time of the birth, once it has thinned out. But for now we don't have to do anything."

As he documented his findings, I assured Dr. Bates that he would be paged for the delivery. Handing the nurse the admission orders, I turned my attention back to Sophia. "I'll be with you every step of the way."

Her mother watched as I massaged Sophia's back and feet over the course of the next several hours. Except for a brief break, my time was spent coaching Sophia through her labor. Sophia's mom continued to glare at me and never left her daughter's side. When the labor pains were coming more intensely every two to three minutes, I announced, "Your labor is progressing very fast, Sophia. You'll feel the urge to push very shortly."

As soon as Sophia began to bear down, I asked the nurse to page Dr. Bates. Upon entering the room, he asked, "How should we do this delivery?"

My reply was standard to every new resident, "Well, I always sit on the side of the bed," and then added, "Sophia seems to be doing a great job pushing right where she is."

"Well, I'd like to do it your way, Marcie," he responded. As the baby's head was getting closer to being born, Dr. Bates repeated, "I think we need to call Dr. Santos. This extra tissue is just not giving way."

"If you'd feel better about getting a second opinion from Dr. Santos, go ahead and call him. I know he's just finishing a surgical case," I replied. Dr. Bates asked the nurse to call Dr. Santos.

Dr. Santos arrived within a few minutes and asked, "How can I help?" Dr. Bates reviewed the situation with him. Dr. Santos explained, "Well, I think we might need to clip that septum. What do you think, Marcie?"

"I'd like to give it a chance to stretch and then see if we can push it out of the way," I answered.

As Dr. Santos left the room, he remarked, "Well, Dr. Bates, you heard her. Do what she says. She's the expert." I stole a quick glance at Sophia's mother. Her eyes were wide and her mouth dropped open with surprise at Dr. Santos' edict.

56

As the baby's head came to a full crown, I pressed the swollen tissue. Fluid oozed out. I pushed the septum out of the way and assisted Dr. Bates with the delivery, my hands guiding his. The spontaneous cry from the baby brought sighs of relief and cheers. Tom cut the cord after the baby was lifted onto Sophia's abdomen. I suggested that Grandma hold her new grandson while we finished the delivery of the placenta and inspected the perineum.

Following the birth procedures, Dr. Bates exclaimed, "That was such a great experience, Marcie! I've never seen that before. You're a great teacher."

Holding her first grandson, Sophia's mother approached me. She put her arm around my shoulders and gave a little squeeze. "I am so embarrassed. Thank you for being here even though I was so ugly to you. You are clearly the expert here. Next time, I'll do more than ask if there's a doctor in the house. I'll *demand* a midwife."

Mother Bear Protection

Lydia provides health care in an urban community clinic serving poor women who often come in with complex social histories. She delivers their babies at the city hospital, fiercely committed to being their advocate every step of the way, no matter what the situation.

"Lydia, I'm giving this baby up for adoption," Jessie told me firmly, even before saying hello. Jessie sat across from me in the exam room, ready for her first prenatal appointment. I had just introduced myself as her midwife.

"Can you tell me what led you to this decision, Jessie?" I asked.

She looked directly into my eyes as she answered, "I have two children already. I'm a single mom and just barely getting by. I can't afford to take care of a third child. This baby deserves a better life. I know deep down that I must give this baby to another family." She paused and checked for my reaction. "The father is not involved," she added. "He knows about the pregnancy and says he doesn't care what I do with the baby."

"I'm sorry to hear he doesn't want to be involved," I responded, then added, "but you can count on me to be with you throughout this whole process." Although this was a conversation that didn't happen every day, it was pivotal for Jessie to hear my support of her plan. "You sound very sure about this."

"Yes," Jessie sighed with some relief, "I am."

Throughout her pregnancy, Jessie never once wavered about her decision. She came to every prenatal visit, each time letting me know where she was with the adoption process. She interviewed a few agencies and then picked one that allowed her to choose the adoptive parents for her baby. Jessie poured over the agency's album, page after page of hopeful couples. Along with a photograph of each couple was a letter explaining who they were, their reasons for adopting, and their goals for parenting. From these pages, Jessie made a list of five prospective adoptive parents, and she considered each one thoughtfully. Finally, Jessie chose Sandy and Karl.

With each prenatal visit and with each measurement of her growing uterus, I talked with Jessie about how she was dealing with her decision to place the baby for adoption. We discussed in great detail the grief that can come with adoption, even when the mother knows deep in her soul it is the right decision. "Allow yourself to grieve," I counseled, "Give yourself the time and space to do that."

Jessie wore large baggy shirts towards the end of her pregnancy. She didn't want her two young children to figure out she was pregnant. She arranged for a girlfriend to take care of them while she was in the hospital.

From day one, Jessie approached the whole adoption process with a mother-bear attitude–fierce in her determination to do what was right for her baby, to take good care of herself during the pregnancy, and to choose the best parents for the adoption. She trusted her strong instincts which provided Jessie with peace about this very personal decision.

One Tuesday morning, as I began my rounds at our hospital's maternity unit, the midwife going off call handed me the list of delivered mothers on the maternity unit. My eyes scanned the list. Jessie's name was at the top. I couldn't wait to see her and hurried down the hall in my scrubs and tennis shoes, my white lab coat flying side to side with each step, and knocked on her door.

"Hey, Jessie, you did it!" I exclaimed. She sat up in bed, looking both resolved and content after giving birth the evening before.

"Yes, I sure did," she replied proudly, "This baby came very fast. And Lydia, I didn't even need any stitches. I feel great!"

We talked through postpartum care and I completed an exam. Sitting at her bedside, I asked, "So, how are you feeling about the adoption plans? Do you have any hesitation or doubts about this? If you do, now is the time to say something."

Jessie again looked right at me, just as she did the first day we met. "No," she answered with continued confidence. "I know this is right and am very comfortable with my decision."

Knowing she would be going home to her other two children and planning to act as if nothing had happened, I reminded Jessie about the grieving process. "'Now remember, it's normal to feel loss and sadness about this baby, even though you know it's exactly what you need to do."

"I get it," she replied. "I promise, Lydia. I'll make time for myself. I have a good friend to talk to if I'm feeling down." I nodded with understanding.

A quiet tap came at the door, and Jessie answered, "Come in." The adoptive parents, Sandy and Karl, slowly entered her maternity room. They stood against the wall to the right of Jessie's bed, as if trying not to intrude.

"Hi, Jessie. How are you doing?" Sandy asked.

As they began to converse, a strange feeling began to churn inside me. No one could tell, but it suddenly grew into a volcano of mixed emotions, erupting from out of nowhere. I continued to sit on the bed, but did not move. The abrupt rush of these intense feelings caught me off guard. Trying to keep my composure, I put myself through a quick internal examination as Jessie talked with the adoptive parents. "What's happening to me? What are all these emotions I'm suddenly experiencing? And why?" I looked down at my crisp white lab coat and blue scrubs, trying to hide the sweat underneath.

Then it hit me. These were the same exact feelings that arose when I brought my new baby daughter home from the hospital. She was a treasure I wanted to hide and protect from the world. I didn't want anything bad to ever touch her life. This instinct with my new baby seemed absolutely sane, yet at the same time, irrational. And now with this new situation, my protective instincts had apparently kicked in once again, this time towards Jessie. "I've just become Jessie's mother bear!" I exclaimed in shock to myself. "Why would this even happen?"

Jessie introduced Karl and Sandy. I mentally jumped from my inner thoughts back to Jessie's maternity room and reached to shake their hands. "Hello. It's so good to meet you." I recognized them from the photo Jessie shared with me when she chose them to be her baby's parents. In person, they struck me as very kind and unassuming, both excited and nervous.

"We can come back later if that would be better," Sandy whispered.

"Oh, no, please stay," Jessie responded.

"I hear you were at the birth last night," I said, trying to make conversation.

"Yes!" they both replied at once.

Then Karl chimed in quickly, "We got to hold the baby right after the birth."

"It was wonderful," added Sandy. Then she looked to Jessie, "You did so well through your contractions and especially during the delivery. You were amazing!"

While observing them interact, I scolded myself. "How silly you are. There is no threat here. These are the kindest, most respectful adoptive parents there could ever be. And furthermore, Jessie certainly doesn't need a mother bear to protect her. She is doing just fine on her own." It was baffling how this protective instinct arose in me from out of nowhere. Despite all rationality and reassurances, these feelings still hovered but were soon replaced by a sense of peace.

After Sandy and Karl excused themselves to go to the cafeteria for a cup of coffee, I asked one more time, "So, are you really okay, Jessie?"

"Yeah," she nodded, "I know it might be hard at times, but this is the right decision for me and this baby. Sandy and Karl will make great parents."

I gave her a hug and one last review of postpartum instructions. We made plans for Jessie to return to the clinic in two weeks and to call sooner if she had any concerns. She agreed.

On my way out the door, Jessie yelled to me as only a proud mama bear could. "Hey, Lydia, you've got to go see her. She's in the nursery, and she's the most gorgeous baby there."

I peaked back in. "You were reading my mind. I'm going to see her before doing anything else."

Entering the nursery, I washed my hands and put on a cover gown. Looking for Jessie's last name on the bassinet, I spotted it in the middle of the

61

room, preceded by BABY GIRL. She lay awake, quietly taking in the noises and lights of the newborn unit. Picking her up, I looked into her deep blue eyes, snuggled her close to my chest, and whispered, "Your mom has made a very big decision for you, and she did it out of love. You are the luckiest girl in the world. Your new parents are wonderful, chosen especially for you. They can't wait to take you home and love you." I paused and repeated, "Your mom loves you very much to do this for you." My mother bear protectiveness surged once again while giving her one last hug. I could hardly put this baby back down in the bassinet.

"What an emotional morning this has been!" I thought to myself, smiling. I bundled her snugly in the blanket and took one last look, imagining the joy she would bring to Sandy and Karl.

Walking back down the hall, I spotted Sandy carrying a baby bag stuffed with supplies and Karl lugging a car seat back to Jessie's room. Yes, I chuckled, it was already starting for them. Their mother and father bear protective instincts were kicking in, right on cue.

Hailey's Hope

Julie is one of two midwives providing obstetric care in a Mississippi river town where choice becomes instrumental in a controversial decision.

"I'll do anything to save Hailey," Therese explained, and then added, "Tim agrees with me."

"Tell me more," I encouraged, sitting back in the exam room chair.

"I really didn't want another child, but circumstances have changed. I want to conceive. If we can collect the baby's stem cells from the cord blood, it might help Hailey in her battle with leukemia. It's my only hope. And I want to be sure I'm healthy before launching into this."

"You're right," I agreed. "Let's make sure you're in good physical shape before you get pregnant." I completed Therese's exam and pronounced her fit. Then we talked through this unique situation in more detail, including the pros and cons. Theresa was determined to see it through. "Come see me as soon as you've missed a period and we'll do a pregnancy test. I hope to see you very soon." Therese smiled.

Ten weeks later, while I was preparing to enter an exam room to do a new prenatal visit, my assistant handed me the chart and rolled her eyes. "This one's a doozy! She's having another baby just so she can collect the stem cells."

Knowing it could only be Therese, I walked in and shook her hand. "Congratulations, you did it!"

"Yes. Thank you," Therese acknowledged. Tears immediately welled up in her eyes and fell gently to her lap. She blew her nose and continued, "I know people think I'm being selfish, but I can't help it. I'll do whatever it takes to save Hailey. Each day I thank God she's still alive. I don't mean to use this baby, but it seems that I am, and it makes me feel guilty." She sighed. "Maybe in time I'll come to love this baby, too."

"Therese, you have such a great love for Hailey. I can't imagine you not loving this child too. Give yourself some time." After completing her exam, I

63

listened for the baby's heartbeat. Hearing the tap-tap-tap-tap-tap started another flood of tears. "What are you thinking?" I asked.

"Death is at my doorstep with Hailey," Therese explained. "She is so ill. Leukemia is such a devastating disease. This baby's heartbeat reminds me how precious life is." She paused, "I desperately want Hailey to live and don't want anything to happen to this baby either."

"I understand. You're very courageous to take on this pregnancy while Hailey is going through chemotherapy." We discussed it further; then, I offered, "If you ever need to talk, please call me. Otherwise, I'll see you in four weeks for your next appointment."

One month later Theresa came to her prenatal visit accompanied by her young daughter. "I'll bet your name is Hailey," I said, entering the exam room.

"How did you know my name?" Hailey asked.

"Well, I've heard all about you from your mom. I understand that you are a brave little girl and that you're going to be the best big sister any little boy or girl could want," I remarked.

Following my comment, Hailey whipped off her hat to reveal her bare head. "Mommy told me I'm going to have a sister and she's going to be bald like me. Is that true?" Hailey inquired.

Delighted by her question, I smiled. "It's very possible, Hailey. This baby will need a hat just like yours. Do you have a spare one?" I asked.

"Yep," she responded. "I have lots of colorful hats for my baby to wear."

I laughed, "You are going to be such a good sister! Would you like to help me measure the baby? Then let's find the baby's heartbeat with this. It's called a doptone."

"Sure," Hailey responded. She climbed up on the exam table next to her mom and listened intently.

From that visit on, Hailey handed me the tape measure and doptone. "You are such an excellent assistant," I remarked.

A couple months later, Therese came alone. I caught my breath and asked, "Where's my helper?" Therese saw my worried look and explained,

"Hailey's white count is low. I couldn't risk exposing her to other people. My mom is at home with her."

"I'm so sorry. This must be incredibly tough," I purposely stated and waited for her reply.

Tears flowed. "It is. I'm finding that people are either very supportive or don't say anything. Some just glare at me," Therese explained. "In such a small town the word is out about what I'm doing. People I don't even know come up to me in the grocery store and start talking about stem cell harvesting. They're pretty bold to tell me their opinion. They also give me a lot of advice about how to take care of myself."

"It is amazing how people stop and talk so freely with pregnant women," I commented. "How about your family? And Tim's? How are they handling your decision to have this baby?"

"Well, they are mostly split about the issue." Therese continued, "Some of them are very judgmental. Despite their opinions, I know I've made the right decision and am doing the right thing. It's also clear in my heart that I'll love this baby deeply, just as much as I love Hailey."

"Therese, it takes a lot of courage to make a decision like this. It's a new concept for most people in this town, in fact, even for this hospital." I continued, "Speaking of that, I'm obtaining information from Hailey's doctors about proper cord blood collection. We've never done this before and we need to make sure we do it correctly. After all, we have only one shot at it!"

At the next prenatal visit, Therese and I concentrated on each step of the procedure. I assured her these details were reviewed with the hospital staff.

Finally, labor began. Therese, Tim, and I met at the hospital. The collection technique was reviewed one last time with the nurses. Even though we had already gone over the instructions several times, we were all still a bit nervous.

The labor progressed very smoothly. Within a couple hours, Hope was born. Her lusty cry filled the room with a spirit of elation and joy, but my celebrating would have to wait. I quickly clamped the umbilical cord to preserve

65

as much blood as possible. The nurse hurried to open the collection kit as I readied the test tubes. Silence permeated the room as I carefully released the clamp. All eyes were on the cord and collection tube. We watched and waited for the blood to start flowing. Slowly the clear container began to fill. I pressed my elbows into my side to steady my shaking hands. "I don't want to lose a drop of this liquid gold." Everyone in the room joined me in a sigh of relief when the final tube was capped.

I turned my attention back to the family and to the newborn, "Therese, what a beautiful baby! Let's see if she is ready to breastfeed. Tim, why don't you go get your mom and Hailey? I'm sure they're anxious to see the new baby."

Within a few minutes, Hailey barged into the room with Tim and his mother close behind.

"Where is she? Where's my Hope?" Hailey beckoned.

I looked to Therese, "Why don't you introduce your daughter to her new little sister?"

She beamed and gave Hailey a big hug. "Hailey, I love you. Meet your sister, Hope."

Hailey moved closer to give the baby a sweet kiss. "Hi Hope. I'm bald, just like you! And when you're home, I've got lots of hats to share with you."

Chapter 3: Life Challenges

Life is never totally smooth. Challenges can arise from all different directions. They can blind side us with their unpredictable nature, throwing our journey off course. They can also lead to new opportunities for growth and understanding. Likewise, how we react to life challenges is simply, a choice.

Hearing in a Different Language

Kathleen is one of two midwives in a budding midwifery practice where she learns to perfect her listening skills.

The beep, beep, beep of my pager broke the silence on that cold, rainy Thanksgiving. I was on my way to a noon gathering with friends for a homemade turkey dinner. The page pushed my mind from neutral into high gear. My heart rate accelerated. I was a new midwife in a young practice, and my director was out of town for the holiday. For the first time, it was just me.

Arriving at my friend's home, I pressed the doorbell and heard footsteps coming to greet me. David and Deanna opened the door and gave me a big hug. Holding up my pager, I promptly explained, "I need to call the hospital right away." Deanna gestured me to the kitchen phone. The aroma of turkey and dressing filled my senses as I quickly punched in the numbers, recognizing the sequence of tones that completed the connection.

Barb, the labor and delivery nurse, answered and informed me, "Marie is on her way to the hospital. Her husband Ben said labor started at six this morning. It's their first child, and it sounds like Marie is in a lot of pain," Barb explained. "They should arrive at the hospital at about one o'clock." She took a breath and added, "By the way, Kathleen, the patient is deaf."

I held my breath for a couple of seconds before responding. My voice hit a high note while exclaiming, "Oh, I see. Well, I'm on my way." My friends, overhearing the conversation, urged me to stay and have a quick dinner with them. "No," I replied, "I need to get to the hospital. My Thanksgiving feast will have to wait. Maybe there will be turkey to eat in the cafeteria. I'll let you know if I can make it back for the good stuff."

Back in my car, I turned the key in the ignition and sat for a moment, thinking about the situation ahead of me. My hands gripped the steering wheel as

I pulled out of the driveway and headed to the hospital. My speed kept pace with my racing heart. I bit my lip while entering the parking ramp.

Turning the car off, I took a deep breath and exhaled slowly, realizing I was in for a double challenge. Caring for a woman having her first baby, for the first time by myself, was one. The fact that she was deaf was definitely the other. Chiding myself for not taking the sign language classes I had always vowed to take, I stepped out of the car and told myself, "Okay Kathleen, get a grip. You can do this. You like a challenge. Here's your opportunity." I whispered a quick prayer, "God, help me get through this one. I'm going to need it." Squaring my shoulders, I walked into the birthing unit.

Barb, the nurse, greeted me and gave an update on Marie's progress and contraction pattern. She further explained that Ben had some ability to hear and he could read lips well. Barb also informed me that the couple was very disappointed that Bobbie, their usual midwife, wasn't on call. With my eyebrows raised, I took in another slow, deep breath and headed for the labor room. "A third challenge," I noted to myself.

Marie's husband, Ben, looked up and smiled at me as I walked in. With a relieved expression on his face, he shook my extended hand. Marie's back was to me, so I quickly moved around to the other side of the bed and bent down. Face to face, I introduced myself while raising my little finger on my right hand and completed a half circle, signifying "Hi." This was the one sign that I remembered after spending a weekend with a friend's deaf parents a few years ago.

"How are things going?" I asked, being sure to speak slowly and exaggerate the pronunciation of each word. Funny, I noticed my voice was a bit louder than usual. I turned to face Ben and asked, "Can you understand me?"

Ben nodded his head yes and said slowly, "Yes, I read lips and can hear as long as you face me and speak clearly."

If I had run across him in another setting, I wouldn't have known he was deaf. I asked, "How should we work together today?" Ben shrugged his shoulders and answered innocently, "I've never done this before. You are the expert!"

69

Smiling, I replied, "I will try my best to stay ahead of you, Marie, but if you need something, just wave or touch me. I will stay within eyesight of both of you. Does that seem okay?" After Ben signed this to Marie, she nodded her head in agreement.

"I know you are disappointed that Bobbie isn't here, but I'll do my best to care for you just like she would," I explained; then I allowed Ben time to sign my words to Marie. She smiled weakly. I watched her response to the next contraction. She closed her eyes and breathed smoothly throughout the contraction, finishing with a cleansing breath. "It's clear you have practiced your Lamaze breathing. You are doing great!" I exclaimed, slowly enunciating each word and waiting for Ben to sign my statement. Placing my hand gently on Marie's shoulder and looking at Ben, I acknowledged, "We will get to know each other very well today. I intend to take good care of you and your baby."

Without thinking, I crossed the room and reached for the knob on the radio, trying to find some soothing music for Marie. I abruptly pulled my hand away and mocked myself, "Just who do you think this music is for, Kathleen?"

Throughout the afternoon and into the evening, I sat in the rocking chair next to the labor bed. Not wanting to leave their side, not even for the cafeteria turkey and stuffing, I munched instead on peanut butter and graham crackers supplied on the unit.

After many contractions, Marie suddenly cried out, "H-E-L-P M-E!" Her monotone voice contrasted sharply with the dramatic expressions usually heard from laboring women.

I responded in shorter sentences while looking to Ben. "You are doing so well. Marie, stay on top of it," I encouraged while rubbing her back. Ben signed my words to Marie. She gave a quick nod.

"T-H-I-S I-S H-A-R-D W-O-R-K," she remarked.

I didn't need Ben to translate my emphatic nod of agreement.

At the peak of the next contraction, Marie grabbed Ben's shirt with her left hand and then pounded on his chest, all while signing rapidly with her right hand. "She wants something for the pain," Ben interpreted, his eyes widening in fear.

I answered, "Let's check your cervix." Following the exam I held up six fingers, "Great progress, Marie!" I began to explain the pain medication options to her and Ben. Maria's brow furrowed as she waved frantically to me and then turned to Ben.

His voice raised a notch, "She wants something now!" It was clear Marie was frustrated with the time it took for Ben to translate all my explanations. I made a mental note to anticipate more so she could be prepared for the next phase of labor. I hurried to find the nurse to administer the pain medications and watched for Marie's response. Her shoulders dropped and her eyes closed between contractions.

The room was silent except for Marie's slow, shallow breathing as she waited for the next pain to arrive. As the nurse listened to the baby's heartbeat, I tapped my fingers on Marie's forearm in rhythm with the thumping sounds. This brought an immediate smile to her face. I shared with Ben and Marie, "This baby has a strong heart–just like his parents."

Over the next several hours, the contractions continued to mount in intensity. I watched for signs that the end of the first stage of labor was near. Remembering the time it took to communicate, I asked Ben to tell Marie, "Soon you will feel the urge to bear down–to push. When you do, please follow my instructions very carefully. There will come a point when I will ask you to stop pushing and then pant, like this." Ben translated and I demonstrated the breathing technique. She nodded her understanding.

Just as I had anticipated for Marie, it was time to prepare for the delivery. Routinely tying a mask around my neck, it dawned on me, "Ben won't be able to read my lips if I wear this." I tossed it in the garbage.

Soon I noticed Marie's abdominal muscles rising and falling with greater intensity. Her face turned red. "Marie, do you need to push?"

There was no need for Ben to interpret Marie's emphatic nod.

71

"Let me see if your cervix is completely open." Ben signed the words to Marie. I held up both hands. "You are ten centimeters. It's time to push."

With each push, the perineum bulged, showing that the baby was descending. "You are doing the right thing," I encouraged Marie. The nurse set up the birthing room just in time. As the head began to appear, I asked the nurse to get a mirror so that Marie could see the progress. Marie looked at the mirror and was amazed to see the baby's black hair. Her dark eyes widened and she sighed an earthy sound, "Ahhhhhhhh."

I gently brought her hand down to touch the top of the baby's head and said, "Soon you will hold your baby–just a little more work." With the next contraction, she pushed even harder and the perineum stretched tight. After the contraction ended, I told Marie, "Look at me now. Small pushes only." Ben signed quickly and she nodded her head.

The room was quiet between contractions. There was just enough time to put a cold washcloth on Marie's forehead. "Not long now," I explained.

"THATS WHAT YOU SAID THIRTY MINUTES AGO," Marie signed to Ben. I grinned, realizing the clock on the wall was in her view.

"Just a little longer–honest!" I reassured her. The room got quiet as she began to push again. "Not so hard, Marie," I yelled, looking frantically at Ben. He quickly signed to Marie. She nodded.

"Just SLOW, easy pushes," I said firmly. "Now a few quick pants."

Even though she couldn't hear me, my voice raised with excitement as the baby's head emerged, "Here comes your baby!"

I reached for Marie's hands and placed them under the baby's arms. Together we lifted the newborn to her chest. Her monotone voice formed the words, "M-Y B-A-B-Y, M-Y B-A-B-Y," as tears streamed down her cheeks.

I exuberantly nodded yes as my own tears fell. "You have a wonderful baby," I said admiringly. She gently rocked her baby, cuddled close to her breast. The silence was broken by a unique display of communication. Loud cheers and tears from Ben and Marie combined with arms, hands, and fingers flying through the air, expressing total relief and great delight. "Marie, you were fabulous!" I exclaimed.

Once things settled down, I stepped out and gave Ben and Marie some privacy with their new child. While completing the paperwork, my rumbling stomach interrupted this momentary lull, growling a resounding "Feed me." My brain responded, "I'm way too tired to feed you the good stuff." Going home seemed a better option.

While warming up the car in the parking lot of the hospital, I pressed my back hard against the seat. The stretch felt so good on my weary muscles. It was midnight. I sighed.

My head hurt, probably due to missing a meal or two, not to mention Deanna and David's Thanksgiving feast. "Yes, it was a hard day, but I met all the challenges," I proudly acknowledged to myself.

Pulling out of the parking ramp and turning slowly onto the empty rain-slicked highway, my hand automatically reached for the radio. Still thinking of Marie and Ben, I quickly withdrew it and headed home in peaceful silence.

That's Just the Way It Is

The transition from a 25-year career in clinical practice to an administrative position is the focus of Maggie's story.

I've made a terrible mistake! Why did I switch jobs now? What the heck was I thinking? Sitting at my new desk, I felt lost before even starting this new job.

Staring at the computer screen, I mumbled sarcastically, "At least I know how to turn the darn thing on." What a feeble effort to build myself up. My notebook was filled with directions from every staff person detailing step-by-step how to do a variety of processes. It included tips on emails, attachments, reports, and simply, writing a letter. *This used to require a piece of paper and a stamp*, I noted to myself.

Not to mention the numerous passwords for this and that, whatever "this" and "that" were. I didn't have a clue. *How is it I can remember details from the thousand babies I delivered, but I can't keep these numbers in my head? Hey, Mr. Computer, are you feeling any pains yet? Boy, I sure am, and they're coming about every two minutes.* As if answering me, the home page appeared on the screen with a sudden beep.

Okay, stop! Take a deep breath. Just get to it. Hey, what can happen? What are you so afraid of? No one's hemorrhaging here. No one needs to be resuscitated. You'd think after twenty-five years of sitting with laboring women, this would be a piece of cake.

It's been a quarter-century of being a midwife and all those years at the same practice. *Aha! That's the last time I had a new job! No wonder this is hard.* I chuckled, remembering back to my first few births. It was nerve racking, watching with an eagle's eye to make sure labor was progressing normally. I'd concentrate on my hand positions as the head made its first appearance and check out the baby carefully while clamping the umbilical cord. And then there was the monumental amount of paperwork. That was a challenge! Just like now. It seemed I should be able to handle this, but I wasn't convinced.

It had taken a long time for me to give up clinical practice and move to this new administrative role. It was incredibly difficult to leave the personal contact with patients–women who inspired me so. I stared at my blank computer screen. *Not quite like my computer buddy here!*

So why did I leave? It began with a stirring, a desire to step back from the focus on my birth center practice to broaden my scope of influence. The longer I practiced midwifery, the more I wanted to deal with the issues that affected midwives across the country. So when this position opened up at our national headquarters, I had to take it.

I played with some paperclips while considering this new development in my life. To be told that this was my job, to have the time to do this work, was such a great opportunity. *I'll be listening to the challenges midwives face and help identify strategies and solutions. It'll help them to know that I was a midwife for twenty-five years. They'll know that I've been in the trenches and understand what they're going through. I'm going to be "midwifing midwives."*

The computer beeped again, as if telling me, "Quit day dreaming and get rolling." *Okay, Maggie, check your email. Send the attachment. Look at your notes. You aren't finding it? It's time to ask for help. Suck it up and just call Katie.*

"Katie?" I asked the administrative assistant in the office next door, "I still don't understand how to do this. Can you please show me one more time?" *Oh boy, this is humbling. The young people here are always going to be 100 times better on the computer than I am. I'd better just accept it.*

Katie eagerly arrived at my doorway. "Sure, Maggie, I can show you. Do you want to write it down this time?" I pulled out my notebook and added instruction #102 to my growing list.

"Anything else I can help you with?" asked Katie.

"Well, let's see. What are some options for formatting this report?" I asked, coveting her knowledge.

Katie patiently proceeded to go through the process step-by-step.

75

"Thanks, Katie. You're a saint!" I said in appreciation. *What would I do without her?*

A couple hours later, I managed to write my first report. *Now to figure out how to save it.* Moving the mouse to find the SAVE option, I simply couldn't find it. *You'd better locate it before you lose all your work! You've heard about those horror stories of people losing hundreds of pages with one wrong click.*

"Katie?" I cried in a panic. "How do I save this?"

"Hold on, Maggie. I'll be right there," she replied so politely.

Please don't erase. Please Mr. Computer, my buddy. Don't lose this report. I beg you!

Once again Katie arrived to save the day and my report. I added instruction #103 to my loyal notebook along with a reminder to bring Katie a treat tomorrow. She deserved an extra reward for all of my interruptions and questions. *Admit it. You're bribing her to keep helping you!*

Somehow, I got through the day and headed home. Walking through the door, I dragged my feet into the kitchen and sat at the island with a big bowl of butter pecan ice cream. Digging in, I found myself repeating aloud the same phrases over and over again, "Maybe I've made a mistake taking this job. What was I thinking? There are so many skills that I don't have."

My 14-year-old daughter Sam overheard me for the tenth day in a row. Previously she sat quietly on the stool and let me vent. But not today. Nope. From seemingly out of nowhere, Sam exploded like a ton of dynamite, "Well, I'm the one who's learning disabled, and I've *always* had trouble in school. This is the *first* time you've ever had a problem like this. So I don't want to hear about it from you anymore. You're the one who is always telling me, 'You just have to deal with it, and that's the way life is.' Now I'm telling you–you're going to deal with it, and you're going to learn how to do this, and that's just the way life is!"

Whoa. I didn't say another word. I set down my spoon and wiped the ice cream from my lips. "You're right, Sam" I told her, embarrassed by my whining. "I hear you loud and clear."

And I did. Just as I learned how to sit with a woman in labor, how to watch her contractions and learn the meaning of her subtle expressions, and how to know when a baby was coming, eventually I mastered the computer, networked with midwives, and provided them with the insight they needed to keep their practices thriving. Most importantly, in this new role, I kept midwives caring for women during pregnancy and birth and throughout their lifetimes.

I've often said, "As soon as you feel like you know everything about obstetrics, something will happen to humble you very quickly." Maybe it's the same with a new job, with computers, or with learning any new challenging skill. It certainly has been humbling–not to mention Sam's repeating of my own words right back at me. Shaking my head and chuckling at this full circle moment, I will always remember Sam's newly discovered voice setting me straight: "You just have to deal with it and that's the way life is."

Baby Blues

A new nurse-midwife, Patti, guides new moms into motherhood in a rural farming community.

I hung up the phone, hoping I had said the right thing. Reviewing my conversation with Betsy, my frustration began to mount. A few days ago, she had delivered her fourth child. In the hospital she had seemed just fine, but just like so many new mothers, Betsy called me in tears. As a new midwife, I didn't expect to be addressing so many postpartum challenges. I felt unprepared. It seemed that for every happy new mother in my practice, there were ten women who were downright sad. Dealing with it all left me feeling depressed as well.

An hour later the phone rang again. I picked it up and listened, hearing only weeping murmurs. Then a quivering voice asked, "Patti? It's me again. It's Betsy. You told me to call back and let you know what was going on. We had to give Kaitlin a bottle because she kept on crying." And then Betsy broke down. She really wanted to breastfeed this baby for a longer period than her other three children. For some reason, Betsy had nursed each of them for only a few days. We had talked about it extensively during her prenatal visits. In the hospital Betsy appeared confident, but breastfeeding had once again become a challenge.

Although it was the focus of Betsy's stress, I wondered what other issues might be contributing to her tears, and probed a bit more. Betsy described how she had cried with all of her new babies and further explained, "I think breastfeeding just makes me more emotional!" I didn't have many words of wisdom. But in some ways, Betsy didn't need any. She just needed to be heard.

Betsy continued on the phone, "Patti, breastfeeding isn't working out again. My nipples hurt. They hurt so much I'm not even wearing a shirt. I don't want my husband to come into the bedroom and see me like this. I feel like such a failure."

"Where is everybody?" I questioned, guessing that her husband was doing farm chores.

78

"Jack is out in the barn, and the kids are here in the house. They seem to be hungry all the time. I should be eating too, but end up cooking for the family. Before I know it, I've skipped another meal."

A click on the phone line caused us to pause. Cows mooed in the background. A male voice said, "Hello?"

Betsy took a deep breath, trying to calm her voice. "I'm on the phone, honey." It was clear she wasn't able to share her feelings with anyone else, not even her husband.

Jack replied, "Oh, sorry hon," and promptly hung up the phone.

I asked Betsy about her husband, Jack, who seemed very sweet to her in labor. Was he helping around the house? Cooking some meals? But I already knew the answer. In our farming community, the gender roles were clearly defined: Jack did the outdoor chores, and Betsy did the housework. It was just assumed. In addition, we lived in a very Catholic community, so birth control was not an option. It wasn't even discussed. In fact, I guessed Betsy was already anticipating a future pregnancy as she held her new baby Kaitlin.

Empathizing with Betsy, I stressed she was not a failure. "Let's talk about some tips that might help the feedings go smoother." At the end of our conversation, I made plans to see Betsy the next morning. Until then, she would try to breastfeed and avoid giving Kaitlin any more bottles. Betsy sounded calmer, but I still felt horrible hanging up the phone.

The next morning at seven, my phone rang again. It was Betsy. "We gave Kaitlin bottles throughout the night. Patti, I can't breastfeed. It's just not working."

I replied, "That's fine, Betsy. I know how hard you've tried. I'm so sorry it didn't work out. You need to know that I support your decision to bottle feed Kaitlin." It still made me sad that Betsy couldn't breastfeed, but it was important she didn't feel shame about it not working out. She needed my complete acceptance and understanding.

The next day Betsy came into my office. As she leaned over the desk, I noticed her breasts were full and engorged, a common condition when breastfeeding has stopped abruptly. I started to ask Betsy more about this. Before I finished my first question, she sat up straight and froze, held her breath momentarily, and squeezed her eyes closed. It was apparent she was having excruciating breast pain. "I can't even bear for this loose t-shirt to touch them," she blurted out and began to sob. She couldn't catch her breath to say a word. I sat down, placed my arm around her and said, "Just let it all out, Betsy. I'm here for you." Her reaction led me to wonder if some depression was also setting in.

After about fifteen minutes, a blank look glazed over her face. She murmured, "What am I going to do?"

Betsy's question flashed me back to a previous patient who had experienced severe postpartum depression. I could never forget her. She had that same blank look in her eyes when she whispered to me, "I don't want to abuse the baby, but I envision throwing him against the wall." It is a thought some mothers experience, but are often too afraid to verbalize. This blank look was one that I've learned to take very seriously.

So I asked Betsy if she had had any thoughts of hurting herself or the baby. "No, not at all," she replied as her eyes met mine. I asked more questions about depression, insomnia, and her appetite.

From our discussion, I assessed that Betsy had mild postpartum depression. We made a plan to get Betsy some help. She began to see a counselor. Over the next few weeks I kept a very close eye on her, touching base by phone every other day.

At the six week postpartum visit, Betsy was doing much better. She described how her kids had welcomed Kaitlin into their family and shared, "The turning point came a couple weeks ago, watching them take turns holding and cuddling the new baby and singing songs to her. For those few moments, everything suddenly seemed right. It's a snap shot in my mind I'll always treasure." She continued, "I also asked my husband to help with a few meals and the laundry so I could rest. And even though I was scared and thought I was asking for a miracle, he was very willing to do that for me!" she exclaimed as if she still couldn't believe it. Betsy was back on track, cherishing the unique moments of motherhood that can rise up out of deep challenges.

Her story stayed with me. It can be so difficult for women to ask for help in this super-woman society of ours. Going home with a new baby can be more difficult than going through labor–not knowing what to expect, being devoted to breastfeeding, changing diapers, losing sleep, feeding other children. Asking for help can feel impossible, especially for women with postpartum depression. Yet new moms like Betsy find their way as they maneuver through this hormonal, stressful, and sleep-deprived period of their lives. Despite it all, they continue on. They hold onto the moments that put it all into perspective–the gift that comes from graciously receiving help from a partner and the bonding of the new family. These new mothers are the true heroes. They are the ones who have inspired and kept me going for the next new mom who calls, softly weeping on the other end of the phone.

Gut Instinct

Debbie is an obstetric nurse in a small town hospital. She listens to her inner voice challenging her to follow a secret dream.

I was attending a church-sponsored fall retreat for women. We sat in a circle on folding chairs and discussed our personal dreams. Karen, my best friend, sat next to me. The facilitator asked, "If you could be anything you wanted, what would you be?"

"I want to be a midwife," I blurted out, surprising even myself. Karen's mouth dropped open as she looked at me in disbelief. I had never shared that piece of information with anyone. Seeing her response, I smiled and looked away, wondering if spilling my guts was a good decision. Now everyone knew my heart's desire. I looked down at my notebook while listening to the other women share their dreams.

The next question raised a lump in my throat and a burning in my eyes. "What is keeping you from achieving what you want to be?"

"I'm busy raising children," came quickly from my lips. Other attendees nodded their heads in agreement. I had two children in grade school and a third enrolled in pre-school. Taking care of my children along with my nursing job took every bit of energy I had. How could I even consider graduate school?

The facilitator then offered several activities to help us develop "next steps" toward achieving our goals. Unfortunately I left the weekend without a clearly defined path. Over the next few years, however, my abrupt declaration at the retreat kept this dream alive, churning in my heart and soul.

Eventually the realities of life seemed to have won over my hopes of ever becoming a midwife. When my youngest child entered third grade, I applied to graduate school at the state university, 150 miles away from home. It wasn't the midwifery program my soul yearned for, but I had rationalized it was a close second option. A good GPA from college, years of experience working as a labor and delivery nurse, and certification as a Lamaze instructor were excellent

82

credentials. Within six months, I received a letter of acceptance into the maternal-child health program at the university.

In September, I drove from our small town into the city for graduate school registration and orientation. The room was full of eager and energized faces. An instructor announced, "If anyone is interested in the midwifery program, please meet with me in the back right corner of the room. We have an open spot." I looked around the room. Coincidentally, I was already sitting in that corner. My gut screamed, "Stay in your chair!" So I did.

When the instructor introduced herself to me, she said that there was one seat available in the midwifery program for the fall semester. She further explained, "A student called this morning to say she was going to enroll at another university."

I stammered, "How often do you have an opening this late?"

"Almost never," she laughed. "Why don't you get some more information from the department secretary. Her office is just down the hall."

The secretary handed me a collection of brochures and introduced me to the director of the midwifery program who had just entered the office. After telling her about my dream and my background, she let me know that there was an opportunity to complete the clinical assignment at a rural practice near my home. I was elated.

Biting my lip, I further inquired, "What about my acceptance into the maternal-child health program? Is there a procedure for withdrawing?"

"Oh, don't worry about it. Mrs. Nelson and I can fix that right away." She offered her hand, "Congratulations! Consider yourself in the midwifery program!" I really liked this lady and her ability to act on intuition.

On the drive home, new concerns bubbled to the surface and spilled out. "Holy cow, I haven't even talked with Bob about any of this. He doesn't even know about my dream to become a midwife, and here I am *already signed up*. What if he isn't supportive? How will I ever juggle the study time with work and taking care of the family? It's a two-hour drive each way, for crying out loud! What the heck was I thinking?" More questions than answers filled my head.

When I arrived home, Bob was waiting for me. He listened patiently as I described my dream and how the day had unfolded. "Honey, honestly, the desire to be a midwife has been in my heart for a long time. I just never thought of it as a real possibility, so didn't say anything. When this opportunity presented itself, I just took it. How could I not sign up? I know I'm asking a lot of you to help make this dream come true."

He started to answer, but I couldn't stop talking. "I don't know how all of this is going to work with the children's schedules and my night shifts at the hospital. When will there be time to study? How will I drive two hours back and forth to classes, especially during the winter?"

Reassuringly, Bob squeezed my hand and said, "Congratulations, darling. You know I'd do anything for your happiness. We'll eventually figure out the answers to all your questions. It might not always be easy, but you're going to become a midwife!"

Little did I know five years ago what a relaxing retreat would have in store for me. Little did I know that one simple question would lead to a gut reaction that would change my life. Launching my new career has been a momentous journey. I love being a midwife. Now when women ask me what they should do about a problem or an issue they're facing, I tell them to listen to their gut. I listened to mine and it was right.

Cleaning Out the Attic

While cleaning out the attic, Nora relives her own poignant story of a marriage and career which took her from the east coast to the Midwest and back home again.

I looked out the kitchen window, sipping my morning coffee. The weatherman's forecast for a hard rainstorm looked accurate this time. Black clouds crawled across the hills, inching their way closer to our country home. A few heavy drops began to tap on the roof. I looked up remembering that cleaning out the attic was on my "to do" list. "Nora," I said to myself, "Today's the day."

And I got to it. Pulling up my hair, I put on some grubby jeans and a t-shirt, refilled my coffee mug, and made my way up the long flight of steps. I reached for the rope to pull down the extension ladder and climbed to the top. Lifting up the attic door, the potential for adventure came over me. I wondered what treasures were waiting to be discovered up here.

I scanned the room, darkened by storm clouds and dusty from neglect. Crossing my fingers I tugged on the chain to the naked bulb in the old ceiling fixture, *not* wanting to go back downstairs for a flashlight. That little errand could distract me from this long-neglected goal. It was time to go through this stuff, relics from a lifetime ago. Luckily the bulb was still good and lit up the space.

Tucked behind a couple of old lamps and a beat up chair, a large leather trunk caught my eye. A likely source of hidden treasure, I lifted the brass handle and gasped. Still wrapped in the gold tissue paper from that last Christmas with Joe were framed family pictures, my family back then.

As I dropped to my knees and slowly unwrapped the first photo, my heart pounded in my throat. I recalled that day long ago, very methodically removing the pictures off the wall, folding tissue paper around them, and carefully stacking each one into the trunk. I could still feel the adrenaline that raced through my veins while packing up the house, struggling to believe this move was really happening. It was New Year's Day and a new beginning for my family, even

85

though it wasn't clear yet where the kids and I were headed. What a range of emotions had emerged at that time, from feeling empowered one moment to feeling overwhelmed and numbed the next. I paused reflectively, grateful to no longer be the woman in that place.

As if in reverse, I unwrapped each framed picture and placed them in a chronological sequence along the wooden planks of the attic floor. "There! There it all is. All laid out." As the wind picked up outside, I took a deep breath. It was too overwhelming to look at them all at once. "Take your time, Nora. One at a time."

I sat cross-legged on the dusty floor, took a sip from my coffee mug, and picked up the first photo. The rain began to pour, tapping against the window pane. Distant lightening flashed, just like the camera as I smiled for this one. There we were, Joe and I, on the Colorado ski trip when we first met. We were there with our friends on holiday breaks from college. I was just a freshman. He was a junior. We were sitting by the lodge fireplace after a day on the slopes. Our faces were red from the sun and still so innocent. That's when Joe asked me, "Where are you from?"

"A Chicago suburb," I replied.

He added, "I have an aunt that lives in a Chicago suburb too."

When I noted that there are a million suburbs outside Chicago, he explained, "Well, she lives in this town called Hampton."

"Wow–I'm from Hampton!" I exclaimed.

He went on, "She lives in this area called Oakland Hills."

"That's where I live!" I said with eyes smiling in amazement. I even knew his aunt who worked at our local grocery store. What an amazing coincidence! What wonderful fate it seemed to me at the time. How idealistic and happy my life was then.

The next photo was Joe standing in front of an African farm. We had been dating for five years, spending much of it apart because of his commitment to Cameroon's agricultural development. A tear collected in the corner of my eye. I was so proud of him back then.

86

And how could I ever forget that Thanksgiving when we got engaged? After all the excitement from our announcement had died down, after the turkey and dressing had been put away, Grandma and I were alone in the kitchen when she turned to me and simply stated, "Nora, don't marry him."

When I asked why, she would only say, "It's the same pattern." I knew what she meant, but couldn't see it in Joe. Not then. Grandma had married my alcoholic grandfather who treated her badly, just like my own father had treated my mother. But I knew Joe wasn't like that. I was different too. I had been to college, after all.

"Ah. Here's our wedding picture." We were so happy and excited that day. It was a beautiful event. All of our friends and family were there. I had just graduated from the nursing program, and Joe was starting law school. It was a day full of new beginnings.

I reached over to view a photo of Joe's parents, sitting stiff and stoic on their thirtieth anniversary. They both died in a car accident four years after our wedding, so we never got to know each other very well.

After the accident Joe started drinking more. It wasn't a problem at first, but it got worse. When he was drunk, Joe became more and more sarcastic and mean. As a courtroom defense attorney, he had honed his natural ability for words. He could filet you like a fish with his comments. And cut to my core he did, even in front of the children. I couldn't do anything right. When he'd come home late from work, the overcooked food would set him off. I felt like a terrible cook back then. "That was the start," I thought to myself, nodding my head. This was when my perception of Joe just didn't jive with his behavior.

Studying the next picture led to another realization, "This was the Joe I thought I knew." He was shaking hands with his new boss, an accomplished attorney with a nationally recognized law firm. This was the last time I saw Joe as a decent, ethical, and fair man. Looking back, it seemed that his position of power at work had accelerated our downward slide.

The photograph of our elegant Victorian home was matted and framed professionally. We had moved to that huge house in a new town when Joe joined the law firm. It was far from my family and friends. I could still see the fear in my eyes as we posed on the rambling porch that summer day. "This is what we've been working for, honey. Relax." Joe soothed me with his usual charm. I had pushed aside my rumbling gut feelings and believed him.

My mind flashed to a winter evening on the same porch later that year. Unlike the welcoming summer day when we had moved in, this particular night was bitter cold and windy. We had been to our minister's home for a potluck dinner. Joe had too much to drink at the small party of church members, embarrassing me. When I mentioned it to him on the way home, he got very defensive and hostile. "You stupid bitch. You have no idea how to have any fun," he snarled. It was twenty degrees below zero and the garage door was frozen shut, so we left the car outside. We stood shivering on the porch as Joe inserted the key into the ice covered lock. It wouldn't budge.

"Please hurry, Joe. I'm freezing," I said. Swearing, he finally got it open. Then, he suddenly turned and pushed me down the steps into a snow bank. While I was laying there absolutely stunned, Joe stepped into the house and shut the door. I heard the loud click of the dead bolt.

"No!" I said under my breath, in shock. Tears flowed down my cheeks, turning instantly to ice. Pulling myself out of the snow and back up to the porch, I pleaded for him to open the door. Looking through the glass I watched him go step by step up the staircase to our bedroom. He didn't even look back despite my knocks on the window.

Finally, our little son Kevin came down the stairs in his feety pajamas. He wiped his eyes, opened the door, and asked, "Mommy, why you out here? It's cold."

I set the picture of the house back on the floor. The rain continued to fall outside, streaming down the attic window. My eyes welled up with tears, thinking about my three kids and all they'd been through.

My hands reached for the photo of Kevin, Lillian, and Joe Jr.–JJ we called him–and clutched it to my chest. Kevin, my youngest, was only two then. I had just started my graduate degree program in midwifery and wanted a picture of all three kids for my wallet. Joe was busy establishing himself in his new law practice. It was my turn to go back to school. Even though Joe had agreed to it, I never felt his full support, especially with three kids to raise. My education seemed to be an inconvenience for him. Looking back on it, he was probably betting that the late nights and intense studies would lead me to give up my dream.

I slid over the wood floor to another large frame, a collage of all my friends back then. There were my midwife classmates hanging out in our school lounge, some neighborhood girlfriends who periodically met for coffee, and the women's group at church. Analyzing this project with new eyes, I realized this collage represented my life separate from Joe. It portrayed my own support system. Maybe it was even an attempt to prove to myself that I wasn't so isolated and my life wasn't so terrible.

While pondering this theory, a new truth arose: my isolation had been self-imposed. I made sure it appeared to the outside world that we had an ideal marriage. It was me who kept the truth hidden. I kept it a secret until Jane came into my life.

There was the picture of Jane and her three kids, almost to the day the same ages as mine. We were in graduate school together. Our husbands were in the army reserves and became best drinking buddies. Jane was the first person I ever confided in. We compared notes and discovered we were facing similar issues concerning our husbands' alcoholic and abusive behaviors. The conspiratorial smile on her face said it all, and from the attic floor, I smiled back. We shared a secret. We had decided to get help together. Although we told our husbands we were studying at the library or going shopping, we instead attended Al-Anon meetings. That was when I realized my behaviors were just as sick, if not sicker, than Joe's. It became clear that although I couldn't change Joe, I could change me.

"Codependency," I said aloud to the spider in the corner. This term was repeatedly defined at meetings: "When you enable the destructive relationship to continue. When you do all you can to protect the abusive person from the consequences of their actions." There were so many things I did to protect the family, to protect our good name, and especially, to protect Joe's reputation.

And then I had to overcome an overwhelming and debilitating sense of shame. I rubbed the back of my neck and shoulder, remembering the burden of all that. It wasn't just the shame of being abused. Joe was having an affair. What a slamming message that had sent me. I had become the poor wife, the boring date, the unattractive partner. Late nights at the office were followed by a few nights when Joe didn't come home. It chipped away at my very core.

I shook myself to change the mood. "Where is that picture?" Scanning the floor, I found the one of me with my kids. Joe hadn't come home that afternoon, or even that night. I had scheduled a special photographer to capture an image of our beautiful family in the rose garden, a new portrait for Joe's law office. I held off crying until after the shoot and then sobbed, waking up the next morning with puffy, swollen eyes when Joe returned through the back door.

Taking a sip of my cold coffee, I could feel tears building and chided myself, "You're really going all out today, Nora. What was that saying about living life one day at a time?" What started as a simple attic project was turning into a catharsis of my soul. It hurt reliving the pain, the shame, and the guilt, remembering how I believed it was all somehow my fault that Joe would do this to me. What a victim I had been.

We tried to go to counseling. What a disaster that was. I have since learned that initial counseling is often not done together when a relationship is abusive. Our sessions provided Joe with more ways to hurt me. After I saw my own therapist, Joe would continually remind me how therapy wasn't working, as if there was never going to be any hope for me, as if I was the only one with a problem.

Then one night, after one more of his cutting remarks, I lost it. I started yelling and screaming at the top of my lungs, completely hysterical. I knew the kids heard it. Their bedroom doors were slamming shut. It all caved in on me–the abuse, the drinking, the adultery, the way he treated the children, and how he physically bullied our sons. I can still hear myself screaming at the top of my lungs, "If you ever touch me or the boys again, I will be out of here with the children so fast you will never see us ever again." I couldn't take it anymore.

After my rampage, all Joe could do was grin and say, "See, I told you the counseling wasn't helping. You're crazy, just like your grandmother and your mother. You'll never change."

Then it hit me. Not only was I acting just like my mother and grandmother, but Joe was acting like my father and grandfather, with his vicious tongue and heavy hand.

At that moment it became clear that things needed to be different. I started reaching out more and was finally honest with my minister, with my church friends, and with my family back home. I told the midwife director at my practice what was happening. Most importantly, I asked for help. I started going to more counseling and Al-Anon meetings. After confiding in people, my life started to lighten up, to feel better. I saw God working through all these other people in my life.

One of those people was Joe's sister Rosie, coincidentally an alcohol and drug counselor. I picked up the photo of Rosie, sitting at her office desk and surrounded by her beautiful orchids. I had confided to Rosie about what was really going on with her brother and me. She shared her insight and wisdom, including years of experience helping families like ours. With Rosie's direction and the help of my minister, counselor, and Al-Anon sponsor, we planned an intervention for Joe.

A professional was hired to run the intervention and confront Joe with his behaviors. We planned to meet in our living room one evening and included the kids, explaining every detail to them about what would happen. If their Daddy did not agree to get any kind of help, I would be asking him to leave our home. And if he didn't leave, I had an alternate plan–the kids and I would temporarily stay with Rosie.

My daughter Lillian had always been an astute young woman, even at the age of nine. Her insight sent shivers down my spine as I prepared a tray of cookies and coffee for the gathering. "Mommy, I don't think Daddy wants to change."

Each one of the kids wrote a note and talked to their Dad during the intervention. Kevin was just seven years old when he so bravely got up from my lap, stood in front of his Dad and asked just one question: "Why did you throw me at the refrigerator?" I hadn't even remembered that particular incident. I recalled Joe picking the boys up by their shirts, slamming them up against the wall and screaming at them, but this refrigerator incident had escaped my mind. JJ sat quietly next to Kevin, holding his little brother as he cried.

Later Joe accused me, "You did a great job of coaching Kevin to say that, didn't you, Nora? Aren't you proud of yourself?"

Joe could not admit to us or to himself that he had a problem. To him, we were all crazy. He refused to look at his behaviors or agree to get help. So I told him he had to leave. Joe looked at Lillian and asked her, "Do you really want me to go?"

She answered, "No Daddy. I don't want you to go, but I think you have to. I think you should just go. You need to go."

Amazingly, he left and never came back. The apartment he had rented for his latest mistress became his new home.

That was probably the bleakest night of my life. Seeing the kids cry as their Daddy walked out with his suitcases tore a hole in my heart, a hole that felt like it would never heal. I sat all night in the dark living room, all alone. Not one light was on. Shadows hovered as I realized that Joe was never going to change. Our marriage was over. All hope was gone.

Back in the attic, I took a deep breath, surrounded by the photos of our home, the kids, and my friends, and began to sob. From somewhere deep inside me came a sorrowful scream that matched the thunderous storm raging outside. All the sad, scared, angry, and hurt feelings from my past erupted and overpowered me. My shoulders shook. Releasing it all, I could hardly catch my breath. Finally, my tears subsided and my breathing slowed. I quietly stared past the photographs through the clouded glass window, seeing a break in the clouds.

My mind still lingered back in time as if looking from the outside in at who I used to be.

Despite my sadness and hopelessness, Joe and I continued a seesaw relationship after he moved out. He filed for divorce and then rescinded his decision. It kept going back and forth. My counselor kept saying, "Nora, You'll know when it's truly over. Trust me. You will know."

Then Joe called one night. He started putting me down and yelled into the receiver, "You are such a lying bitch! You stupid whore!"

That's when my inner voice finally spoke up. "You don't ever have to listen to this again." I finally knew and hung up the phone.

After that, an awareness of my own personal power clicked into place as fast as a line of dominos falling into an intricate pattern. Before this, I always felt powerless. I was the woman having things done *to* me. I was abused, cheated on, and there was nothing I could do about it. Then it came to me. I had power. My husband was in a very vulnerable position. He was a prominent and public person with a professional reputation to maintain in the community. He could not afford to have the police called, appear in a newspaper headline, or endure a tarnished image. With this insight, it became clear I could make a better life for my kids and me.

I got that divorce and moved us closer to my family. My midwife director gave me a letter of recommendation for the new practice I was joining. My kids adjusted well to their schools and made new friends.

"I did it," I said softly to myself, then repeated the words in a voice that echoed throughout the house: "I did it!"

My coffee mug was empty. I looked at my watch. It was nearly two o'clock. I curled up with a quilt in an old brown chair and fell into a deep sleep. A couple hours later, I woke to sunlight pouring in through the attic window. The storm had passed. A healing had taken place in this old musty attic.

I got up, my legs wobbly from sitting for so long. Still a bit groggy, I lowered myself down the ladder, took the stairs back down to the kitchen, and passed a new group of photos on the wall of my home: my grown-up children, my family, an older Rosie still surrounded by her orchids, a reunion photo with Jane, and my loving husband, Greg.

The phone rang, jolting me back to the reality of the day. I heard Greg's tender voice, calling me long distance from his job site. "Hi, sweetie, I was just thinking about you. What are you up to today?"

I smiled and explained, "Oh, I finally got up to the attic. I traveled back in time and cleaned up a whole mess of old cobwebs. And," I added, "It feels good."

"Did you happen to find any treasures along the way?" he asked.

"Oh, yes!" I replied confidently, "I most certainly did."

Birth of a Midwife

Born on a commune, Brianna grew up with a natural view of childbirth. One particular experience during midwifery school forces her to reevaluate this life-long perspective.

It all started on a warm sunny day at Shady Creek commune where I grew up and fell in love with birth. While the other kids were running around the yard, screaming and yelling in a game of tag, I sat alone, remarkably quiet and focused for a four-year-old. I was perched on the top step of the old summer kitchen–a screened in porch separate from the main house. In years gone by, this room was used for canning and large quantity food preparation. On this particular day, a miracle was taking place.

A doctor had come to help one of the women deliver her baby. She was laboring in this summer kitchen where the warm, fresh breezes could flow through from all sides. Even though you could see through the screened windows, I didn't want to look in on something that seemed so private. So I sat with my back to the door, my eyes closed. Concentrating hard, I strained to hear what was going on inside, but the only sounds were whispers. "I wish those kids would quit making so much noise!" I thought. Suddenly, through the screen door, the soft murmurs of a new baby wafted, sounding not terribly different from a newborn lamb. I was hooked, fascinated by birth from then on. Birth was a frequent occurrence and a very natural part of my life at the commune.

Kelly, who also lived at Shady Creek, delivered her first baby there. She was generous, warm, and open. Kelly included me in her life as if I were one of her own children. I would wake up in the morning and join her in their family bed, watching closely as Kelly breastfed her newborn. She talked on and on about how fabulous motherhood was for her. That sealed it. I fell in love with the whole package: pregnancy, birth, and breastfeeding.

During my early teen years, my parents divorced and we moved off the commune. My father remarried, and soon after, he and his wife were expecting their first child. Even though I lived with my mother, my dad and step-mother encouraged me to be involved with their pregnancy and took me to childbirth classes with them. They welcomed me at the birth. I sat patiently in the waiting room until the announcement came, "Brianna, it's time." I stood in the birthing room doorway in the embrace of a close family friend. "Wow!" I exclaimed, observing my sister's entry into the world, feeling so special to be included in this intimate moment. It looked easy and wasn't scary at all.

In my later teens, I worked as a candy striper at our local hospital's obstetric unit. I regularly visited the new mothers and often stayed hours later than expected. It felt comfortable and seemed like a second home. My mom was always there to pick me up, no matter how late it was.

I progressed from candy striper to nursing student to obstetric nurse, and finally, to becoming a student midwife. Every step of the way, Mom always said, "You can do it. Brianna, you can do whatever you want to do." Out of the blue one day, she added emphatically, "And call me if you ever have any tearful days."

"How did she know?" I later thought to myself. Sure enough, one of those days came in midwifery school. My favorite patient had just experienced a horrendous birth. During her labor, this lovely woman experienced a flashback to her childhood and a memory of being sexually molested. She had shared this part of her history with me during the pregnancy. During her contractions, she kept saying, "Don't touch me! No! No!" Although her eyes were open, it was as if she was somewhere else. She couldn't see us in the labor room with her. Not even her husband, who tried so desperately to bring her back to the present, could get through to her.

I kept whispering, "You're safe. You're here with us having your beautiful baby." But she didn't respond. I couldn't calm her. I couldn't take her memory away. Nothing worked. She didn't react to our instructions when it was time to push her baby out. The physician was so kind and patient, but eventually he had to apply forceps to deliver the baby. Her screams during the birth echoed in my mind as I walked down the long hospital corridor, through the automatic doors, and out to my car. With tears spattering my face, I sat down in the driver's seat and sobbed. Trying to make sense of what just happened, I asked God, "What am I supposed to learn from this?"

I thought back to Shady Creek. All my life, birth had been normal and smooth. From these events it became my belief that as a midwife I could have a positive impact on a woman's birth experience, and in many ways this was true. Then a deeper realization hit. I had mistakenly assumed that I could prevent women from ever having a bad birth experience, that somehow this could be controlled for all of my patients at all times. "How arrogant I've been!" I scolded myself. And it hurt. It was painful. It was hard to give up an ideal that I had unconsciously held onto for so long.

Still sitting in the car, I called my mom. As she listened, I was able to accept this basic truth: There are many situations in life over which I have no control, including obstetrics. How obvious this was to me now. With my acceptance came a sense of freedom from this self-imposed, unrealistic standard.

After I graduated and joined a rural practice, I developed new fears. In this more isolated environment it would be especially vital to step up and handle the rare complications that would eventually arise. Again, I called Mom. She was very straight forward with me. "You're right. Emergencies are going to happen. There will be problems, even bad outcomes sometimes. There will be complicated births. Much will happen that is totally out of your control. And you, my dear daughter, are going to do the very best that you can, even in the midst of such challenges."

Her honesty made me feel like she really knew me. Despite my impressions growing up, birth doesn't always happen easily. I acknowledged to myself, "Of course. Yes. How simple. You are so right, Mom. Thanks."

It all started at Shady Creek Commune. Because of the people who raised me, birth has always been a part of my life. Because of midwifery, birth will always teach me about life.

Next to Joe's

Loretta welcomes her first patient at a Native American clinic, located in the midst of a busy city neighborhood.

"How is anyone ever going to find this tiny storefront clinic?" I wondered.

Melinda, the nurse, seemed to have read my mind. "Look for the Joe's Steakhouse sign," she explained to a new patient on the phone. "We're right next door." Just then Renee walked in, on time for her first prenatal visit. I was impressed. Someone had actually found us!

Renee was the first patient at our American Indian Clinic. She signed herself in and sat down on one of the three chairs that made up our lobby. Melinda called her name and instructed Renee to sit in an old office chair that came with the place, the dark wood finish smoothed from years of use. Despite the cramped work area, Melinda skillfully organized Renee's chart, asked a few questions, and checked her blood pressure and pulse. She accompanied Renee down a short narrow hallway to our only exam room.

"Loretta, she's ready for you," Melinda stated as she handed me the chart. "It's her second pregnancy."

I walked in, introduced myself, and sat practically knee to knee with Renee. The exam table took up the majority of space. She was a petite Native American woman with tired brown eyes and straight ebony hair.

"I'm so glad you're here," I said, "How are you feeling?"

"Okay," she responded quietly, looking down at the wide plank floor.

"Do you have any questions or concerns before we start to review your health history?" I asked.

"No," Renee provided another one-word response.

She gave brief answers to my questions about her medical history. After asking about her last menstrual period, I showed Renee the pregnancy wheel and her likely due date.

98

"And what about the baby's father?" I paused. "Is he involved?"

"He's not around," she answered immediately, "but I plan to keep this baby."

We moved on to more questions about her health habits. "Do you smoke, Renee?"

"Yeah," she replied, "about a half pack a day."

I talked about the risks of smoking during pregnancy and gave her some tips on how to cut down and eventually quit. Then, I asked about alcohol and drug use.

"I've been drinking," she admitted quietly. Renee looked up at my face, checking for my reaction.

"Let's talk about it," I replied calmly.

Renee went into more detail and explained that she was drinking on a regular basis. "I'm scared it might hurt the baby, but...." Her voice trailed off.

She was being so honest with me. It was important to pick my next words carefully, to provide support and also be truthful about the effects of alcohol on her developing baby. Motivating her to make a change and stop drinking became my number one priority. I knew in my heart this could be a daunting task, even for a newly pregnant mother. The prevalence of alcoholism was high among Native Americans. It was vital not to come across as judgmental.

She listened closely to my explanation of fetal alcohol syndrome and all its varied effects. I pushed on and discussed some resources that were available, from the local hospital to a nearby outpatient program and Alcoholics Anonymous.

Handing Renee a couple brochures, I encouraged her to make a change. "The best thing you can do for your baby is to stop drinking alcohol completely." She didn't say much more after that. I finished her history, completed her physical, and ordered the prenatal lab work. "Here's the midwife 'on call' phone number for you if any questions or concerns come up before your next appointment, ok? We're available twenty-four hours a day. Call anytime you need to. And Renee, I'd like to see you back here at the clinic in two weeks."

99

This was someone I wanted to see more frequently than once a month. She scheduled her next appointment and walked out. From the front window I watched Renee cross the street and wondered, "Did anything we discussed today get through to her? I surely hope so."

Two weeks later, Renee did not show up for her appointment. Melinda tried to call her at home, but the phone line was disconnected. We sent a letter reminding her to make a new appointment. The envelope was returned a few weeks later with NO LONGER AT THIS ADDRESS stamped across the top. A couple months passed and we still heard nothing from Renee–no response, no phone call, nothing.

"Where could she be? Is she still drinking? Will we ever see her again?" These questions continued to nag me over the next few months.

Another clinic day arrived. I parked my car in the parking lot behind the row of storefronts. The cook from Joe's Steakhouse stood at the open back door of the kitchen, having a smoke. The aroma of steak and fries followed me into the back door of our clinic.

"Your first patient is in the room already," Melinda informed me with a knowing smile.

I walked in and was instantly startled. There sat Renee. I exclaimed, "Oh, Renee! We've been worried about you. Where have you been?"

"I went to rehab," she asserted without any hesitation. Her voice remained quiet but revealed a tone of newfound confidence and excitement. Renee looked up at me and added, "I couldn't wait to tell you."

Her expression was sparkling with pride. She continued, "I was there for two months. They said I could try outpatient treatment, but I *knew* it had to be in-patient. I'm clean. It's because of what you said. This was something I had to do for myself and for this baby."

"Oh, Renee, I'm so proud of you!" I exclaimed.

She shared her future goals. "I want to be a good mom to this baby. I want to give him a good home." This was a new Renee sitting in front of me with a radiant light in her eyes.

100

Renee came to every prenatal visit for the remainder of her pregnancy. She went into labor one day before her due date and delivered a healthy boy. She got a waitress job at a nearby diner, an alcohol-free hangout for alcoholics wanting to stay sober. Melinda and I would stop in periodically for lunch and touch base with her. Renee continued going to AA meetings every week. She returned to the clinic each year for her annual exam. During these visits Renee told me all about her kids and brought photographs for me to hang on my refrigerator at home. Periodically I got a call from her with a health question. And no matter what, she always told me exactly how long she'd been sober.

Renee was the first patient to find our tiny clinic. Here she discovered the courage to face the dark shadows in her life and relight the flame in her soul. She found her true self again and started a new life, thanks to our humble little space next to "Joe's Steakhouse."

Full Steam Ahead

Beth is extremely proud of her ability to advocate for women in her rural practice even when it has the potential to get her into hot water.

Her question blew me out of the water. I've always encouraged my patients to ask whatever questions they had, but this one hit me like a tidal wave. "I want to have a water birth this time. It's *got* to help my chronic back pain." Nancy looked right at me and pointedly asked, "Can you make this happen?"

Nancy's unexpected request took me by surprise. I took a quick, deep breath and responded, "Well! I certainly wasn't expecting you to ask that. There's never been a water birth at this hospital before, but there's always a first time for everything. I've read about it, but will need time to do some studying on the topic."

I grinned, "This might get me into some hot water here, but we've got nothing to lose by making a request. However, we have to be very prepared if we're going to be taken seriously. Nancy, here's your homework assignment: I'd like you to find out where you can rent a birthing tub because I have no idea where to look. I'll work on getting the research to support this."

Nancy's enthusiastic resolve prompted me to plunge into my homework, ordering a literature search on water birth through the medical library. My next strategy was to discuss the issue with the nurse manager of the obstetric unit. I would definitely need her on my side before approaching the physicians and was relieved to find her so receptive and supportive of the idea. "Just be sure to gather plenty of sound evidence if you want to convince the docs," she advised.

At Nancy's next prenatal visit I reported the results of my literature search. The studies provided evidence of positive outcomes from water birth that would be very difficult to ignore. I further shared with Nancy that the nurse manager supported the concept, "I'm so excited about her response. She is an important ally. Now tell me what you've learned about the tub."

"I have at least two options for tub rental. Each company is sending me quotes and then we can decide on the better choice," Nancy reported.

"Well, we're picking up steam to keep this engine rolling," I asserted. Nancy smiled.

At her sixth-month check up, I told Nancy about the National Center for Water Birth. "I'm registered for their conference at the end of this month and so excited to learn more about this option for your labor."

"Well, I've been in contact with one of the water tub rental companies," Nancy explained. "They're willing to rent the tub to me, but the cost is pretty steep."

"Here's an idea," I began. "I'll write a letter to your insurance company detailing the causes of your back pain. Maybe they will reimburse you for the expense."

"That would be great!" Nancy replied.

"Consider it done. They can only say 'yes' or 'no.' It never hurts to ask," I responded. "In the next couple of weeks, I'll be presenting your request for a water birth to the nurses and the doctors. I'm armed with a boatload of good research and will let you know what happens at your next visit."

Nancy jumped when I entered the exam room a few weeks later, "What happened when you talked with the staff?"

"It was interesting," I explained. "The nurses were skeptical at first, but in the end they were receptive. After hearing my presentation, they wanted to do some more reading. I came prepared with a list of online articles and websites. They're also going to watch the video I purchased at the water birth conference. In a couple of days, I'll meet with them again and answer any questions they might have."

Nancy inquired, "And the doctors?"

"Well, I was kind of expecting the proverbial 'wet blanket,' but was pleasantly surprised. Although they weren't exactly enthusiastic, they were not altogether closed to the idea either."

103

I continued, "With all the evidence I found to support water birth, it's difficult to dispute. Not one of the doctors said, 'Over my dead body will you do a water birth,' so that's a positive sign. They seem to be taking a wait-and-see position, and hopefully we'll get to set the precedent. Sometimes it takes a lot of conversation before a major change can be accepted. I also finished writing the protocols for water birth. Who knows, maybe this will become a routine option for labor and birth here."

"Well, I've got some good news," Nancy declared.

"Let's hear it!"

"I heard from the birthing tub company, and the tub is on its way. Here's the best part. I talked with the insurance company and they're going to reimburse me for the tub rental!" Nancy glowed with her good news.

"That's great! More than I ever expected. And all this from simply asking for what you need. You certainly got me fired up about the topic. We've jumped over all the hurdles I can think of. Now we just need to wait for labor. Be sure to call me early when you go into labor so we can get everything set up."

Three days before Nancy's due date, my phone rang at one o'clock in the morning, "Beth, I'm definitely in labor, and it's all in my back." Waves of tension filled her voice.

"Let's head to the hospital," I directed. I called Labor and Delivery informing them we were on the way. The charge nurse who took my call was delighted, "Wait until everyone hears about this. We'll get things flowing!"

Arriving at the hospital, I found the nurses filling the tub for Nancy. She was pacing in the labor room and pleaded, "Please hurry. I need the warm water. The contractions are breaking my back." She stopped long enough to notice me. "Boy, am I glad to see you!"

Assessing the water level, I encouraged Nancy, "Pretty soon the tub will be full and then you can relax." Teasing, I added, "Before you make your big splash, let's listen to the baby's heart rate."

Fifteen minutes later I reviewed the monitor strip, "The baby looks good. Let's get you in."

104

Nancy's husband Eric steadied her as she entered the water. Quickly, she brought her other leg in and submerged herself. Within minutes Nancy proclaimed, "Oh my, this feels marvelous." Her easy steady breathing and gentle smile confirmed that the warm water helped her relax and work better with the contractions.

After spending several hours immersed in the water, Nancy gasped, "Beth, I think the baby is coming. I need to push!"

"Okay, let me get my long gloves on first, before you start. Do you remember how to puff through the contractions?"

I quickly got my shoulder-length gloves on and positioned myself on kneepads at the side of the tub. I checked to see if Nancy was completely dilated and found the baby's head ready to be born.

I instructed the nurse, "Please make sure the baby warmer is ready, just in case we need it." I coached Nancy, "We're ready any time you are, Nancy. You can go ahead and push with your next contraction. Let's ease this baby into the world."

Nancy's abdomen raised and lowered with each push. Soon the baby's head emerged from the birth canal and rested in my hands. I continued my coaching. "Nancy, one more push for the shoulders to be born." With the next contraction, Eric plunged his hands in the water with mine, and we brought the baby up out of the water and placed him between Nancy's breasts. The nurse quickly dried him off with a warm blanket.

Nancy cried, "Oh, look." We watched in awe as the baby opened and closed his eyes several times and then made a soothing cry.

I was elated and amazed at how the warm water had helped Nancy through her labor, especially with her back problem. Cheering and clapping came from outside the door. All the labor and delivery nurses and obstetrics residents were standing in the hall.

Directing the next step, I said, "Nancy, let's get you into bed while we wait for the placenta to be delivered." When the rest of the birth procedures were

105

completed, Nancy was propped up with pillows and Baby Marc was nursing like a little champ.

Nancy's eyes glowed, "Beth, thank you so much. I wasn't sure you would take my request seriously, but you made it happen."

I had to give her the credit. "No, Nancy, you're the one who started the fire and got me all steamed up for this project. I'd say we made a big splash here today! And it's sure to whet everyone's desire to offer water births to our future moms."

Holiday Headlines

As snow fell outside a suburban women's clinic, Claire sat inside and debated making a phone call to her patient the day before Christmas.

"ABNORMAL" was stamped in red ink across Helen's mammogram report. There was no question about these results. It was as clear as the black print on white paper, and it was very serious. Unfortunately it was also Tuesday, the morning of Christmas Eve. Staring at the report in my hand, I realized I was holding much more than a piece of paper. I was holding Helen's future, a glimpse into her New Year.

"Do I call her today? Please let the answer be no," I debated with myself. A traditional Christmas scene came to mind—a fireplace crackling, turkey dinner on the table, presents under the tree. "This news will ruin Helen's Christmas," I tried to rationalize.

My inner voice responded with a fiery truth, "This is her body." That phrase alone guided my thinking. I wanted to protect Helen from this information for just another day and a half, until after the holiday, but waiting would delay the urgent follow-up that was so strongly indicated. My inner voice persisted, "This is her body. She has a right to know what's going on. She has phone calls to make."

I quickly reviewed my calculations, factoring in the number of days medical offices would be closed over the holidays. If I waited until Thursday to call Helen, it would be the following week before she would see the surgeon. If I called her today, there'd be a good chance she'd get an appointment by the end of this week, maybe even the day after Christmas. "I can't wait, not even for this special celebration," I concluded.

I picked up the phone and then set it back down. "Where's her phone number again? There it is, right there in her health records." I procrastinated, trying to think through the right words to say, and sighed deeply. No one ever taught me how to give a woman abnormal test results on Christmas Eve. "Just be straight with her," my mind instructed.

107

My fingers dialed the phone number. It rang twice. "Hello?" Helen answered.

I closed my eyes for a moment, dreading having to tell her the news, especially on this particular morning. "Hello, Helen. It's your midwife, Claire."

Helen paused. She knew I had ordered her mammogram and it was the only reason I would be calling.

"Yes?" she asked hesitantly.

"I have some news for you that we need to discuss." I paused momentarily. "I'm going to be very honest with you, Helen," I said, trying to prepare her. "And I wish I didn't have to call you, today of all days."

"It's my mammogram result, isn't it? What's wrong?" she asked.

"Yes, Helen, it is. The results are not normal. The report describes an area of breast tissue that needs more testing. You need to see a surgeon for follow-up as soon as possible. You'll most likely have an ultrasound and then a biopsy to evaluate this finding more directly."

"There. I said it," I thought to myself.

Then I elaborated, "Helen, I'm so sorry to call you at this time and wish it could have waited until after Christmas. But I didn't want to delay scheduling this important appointment."

Helen agreed wholeheartedly and we discussed the plan further. "I've forwarded your mammogram report to the surgeon. Do you have a pen and paper? They're ready to set up an appointment for you. This is the number to call. You need to be seen within the next few days–the sooner the better."

I explained in more detail which procedures the surgeon would likely perform. She had no questions. "Helen, try to take this one step at a time. I'll be thinking of you. Please keep me posted, okay? This will surely be on your mind, but I hope you'll be able to enjoy your Christmas."

"Thanks, Claire. I will," she answered quietly.

Hanging up the phone I questioned, "Did I do the right thing by calling her today?" and then answered half-heartedly, "Yes, I think so." This situation continued to haunt me.

New Year's came and went. I was back in the office seeing patients when the phone rang at my desk. Helen spoke, "Claire, it was breast cancer," she told me, not mincing her words. "I've already had surgery and I'll be starting chemo in a couple weeks."

"Oh, Helen, I'm so sorry," I responded. We talked in detail about everything ahead of her. Helen sounded amazingly calm considering what she had already been through and what she was still facing.

"You know, Helen," I shared, "It was a struggle the morning of Christmas Eve, trying to decide whether or not I should call you that day. I didn't want to ruin your holiday. But with the results of your mammogram, I knew it couldn't wait."

"It's a good thing you didn't wait. Claire, you did the right thing to call me that morning," she reassured me.

"Thank you," I answered, feeling like she had just given me a gift.

Later that week I reviewed a pathology report which verified the specific diagnosis of Helen's breast cancer. Since the surgery had been scheduled so quickly, Helen's long-term prognosis was very positive. The cancer had not yet invaded her lymph nodes, but the surgeon removed some of the surrounding tissue to be extra cautious. The chemotherapy Helen would receive was mostly cautionary to ensure that any remaining malignant cells would be eliminated.

Listening to my inner voice helped me deliver this holiday news, information that allowed Helen to write her own headlines for this New Year.

Chapter 4: Life Humor

What would life be like without humor, that intangible necessity that can pull us out of a funk and keep the sparks flying? These stories will touch both your heart and you funny bone. Go ahead–allow yourself a gut wrenching laugh!

Perfection to Powerhouse

Jackie is one of the founding midwives of an east coast birth center where she observes the births of many "powerhouse women."

Sylvia looked like a magazine cover model. Not one hair was out of place. Her makeup was impeccably applied, and her nails were well-groomed and polished. She wore stylish clothes accessorized with color-coordinated shoes and a handbag. She was college-educated and had married her high school sweetheart. Sylvia followed the rules. And she was pregnant with her first baby.

Sylvia was also a study in contrasts. Following her first obstetric visit with me a month ago, I knew she would be different from our usual, more assertive birth center patients. During her second prenatal appointment, she sat in front of me with her legs crossed tightly and hands folded on her lap, looking down at her sleek shoes. "How are you feeling today, Sylvia?" I asked gently.

"I'm okay, Jackie," she murmured in a quiet whisper.

"Do you have any questions?" I inquired routinely. Frequently, our birth center patients would pull out a long list from their purses.

"No," she answered, glancing at the door as if planning her escape.

"Have you thought about breastfeeding your baby?" I asked, trying to start a conversation.

"I don't know if I could do that," Sylvia responded with a slight southern accent.

I thought to myself, "Oh boy. She is afraid of her own shadow."

"Let's take a listen to this baby's heart beat," I said, hoping to give her something positive to remember from today's visit.

Moving to the exam table Sylvia stood up, five feet and ten inches tall. With her charm-school posture and heeled sandals, she towered over my short frame. I made a mental note. "Aha! Tall women like this usually deliver easily."

Gently lifting her summer top, I placed the fetal doppler onto Sylvia's slightly bulging lower abdomen. The amplified "thump thump thump" of the

112

baby's heart beat filled the room. I smiled and looked for Sylvia's reaction. Instead of smiling back, she stared at the ceiling and remarked, "How am I ever going to be a good mother?"

"Oh my," I thought to myself. We talked through Sylvia's concerns, and I did my best to reassure her, even trying some humor. "You know, Sylvia, if you weren't worried about being a good mother, I'd have to worry about you!" I said with a chuckle. She maintained her serious composure.

Fall arrived with a chill in the air. Picking up the next chart and calling Sylvia's name, I scanned the notes from her previous appointments with the other midwives in our practice. Sylvia leaned from one side to the other as she rose from the lobby chair, placing her hands on a table to keep her balance.

"Have you ever grown!" I exclaimed, "And you're due in a couple weeks already." She lumbered into the exam room. We sat down, and I asked, "So, how are you feeling about labor, Sylvia?"

"Oh, Jackie," she replied, "I'm so scared. I can't do it. It's going to be terrible."

Sylvia explained that the childbirth classes she and her husband attended made her even more fearful of birth. "What will it be like when I don't have an epidural like all of my friends? How am I going to do this in the birth center without one?"

I pondered her questions in my mind. Sylvia had developed fears about birth that seemed more ingrained in American women than their global counterparts. Just the day before, one of our birth assistants from England had excitedly called her mother overseas to tell her that she would be having her baby at the birth center. Her Mom had responded, "Oh Annie, I'm so sorry to hear you can't have a home birth." What a completely different message these mothers were giving to their daughters, compared to the hospitalized, anesthetized image conveyed to our daughters here in the States.

"Let's talk about your fears, Sylvia. And, let's talk about epidurals." I continued, "They may take away the pain for a while, and sometimes they are necessary, but epidurals have their share of risks, too." We discussed her feelings

113

in detail.

Sylvia's husband Steve joined her for the following prenatal visit. He sat quietly and watched without asking questions. I measured Sylvia's abdomen and checked her cervix, which was beginning to open and thin out.

"It might be quite soon," I told them. After describing the symptoms of early labor, I tried to reassure and encourage Sylvia, "You're going to do great!"

"I don't know about that," Sylvia murmured, shuffling her feet out the door.

A week later, Sylvia was first on my schedule. I looked into the waiting room, expecting to see her downcast eyes and ever-enlarging abdomen. Instead, Sylvia looked me right in the eye and exclaimed, "Jackie! Look at what I did!" She lifted up her new son and beamed. I also noted that Sylvia held her chin a bit higher than she did the week before. As we talked in the exam room, she placed her new son to her breast. He sucked vigorously.

"Oh, my goodness! I'm gone for just a couple days and look what happens. You're here for a post-partum visit! How was your labor?" I asked.

Sylvia described every single detail. She explained that the baby came so fast that the midwife almost didn't get her gloves on in time. I nodded my head, recalling my theory about her height. She continued to breastfeed like a pro while she pulled out a list of questions to ask about the baby.

"Is this really Sylvia?" I asked myself. "This can't be the woman I was worried about last week, because it's very clear *this* new mother is going to be just fine. What a transformation!"

Over the next five years, I continued to see Sylvia at the birth center for two subsequent births. She continued to shine and enjoyed being a mother. One day, while entering the front door, I noticed a tall woman holding a baby on her hip with two young children at her side. She spoke firmly but lovingly to them, very much a mother in charge.

She looked up and yelled my name, "Jackie!" It's me–Sylvia!" She opened her free arm to include me in a big hug. "I'm pregnant again! Baby number four is on the way!" she proudly announced.

"This is becoming quite the routine, Sylvia!" I teased, "Let's go downstairs and start your prenatal care. You probably don't even need to fill out any forms. I should have your health history memorized by now!" Sylvia laughed easily.

"I'm glad to be back again," she told me. "It feels like home." She wore blue sweats and not a smidgen of make-up. Her scuffed tennis shoes were dusty with dirt from her garden. Sylvia's hair was hastily stuffed into a clip. Her once manicured nails were neglected and chipped. But Sylvia was even more beautiful than ever. She was radiant and self-confident, emitting a spirit of inner strength and a passion for life.

Her thick chart flipped open to my notes from her initial prenatal visit during her first pregnancy.

I pointed to my original written entry and showed Sylvia, "You'll get a kick out of this. Look here: 'Appears nervous and shy.'"

Sylvia read my mind and questioned, "Do you remember what I was like back then?" She threw her head back and howled with laughter.

The pure joy in Sylvia's face led me to a moment of reflection. Sure, it's fun to work with pregnant women who know exactly what they want in labor–a jacuzzi, the freedom to move about and change positions, all those specific requests that come with a detailed birth plan. I don't have to do a thing. I just smile and say, "Oh, you're going to be great in labor!"

But the real exciting part of being a midwife is to watch someone like Sylvia transform from a scared shadow into a radiant, confident, powerhouse woman and mother through the miracle of childbirth. As a midwife, I've watched these women successfully give birth and grow in amazing ways from the experience. And I say to myself, "Ahhh. Good. There. Another one. Another new mom who will be okay. Just like Sylvia."

115

He's Mine

Mary is a student midwife from Pennsylvania who learned to deliver babies along with a punch line.

Kim closed her eyes and rested her head on the pillows as she recovered from the last contraction. Her breathing was slow and rhythmic, signaling that the pain medication was having its full effect. Kim, a twenty-six-year-old math teacher and Gary, her architect husband, were about to deliver their first child. Gary, wide-eyed, lurked quietly over her shoulder. Their familiar world of algebra and blueprints were an eternity away.

Kim frowned as the next contraction began. She took in a slow deep breath. With the next exhale, she pulled her legs up, tucked in her chin, and grunted in a low tone, "Uuuhhh, uuuhhh, uuhh."

Gary whispered to her, "Keep pushing, honey."

I encouraged her, "You're very close to having your baby. Just a few more pushes." I scanned over to Tim and noticed the color leaving his face. "Tim, you look a little pale. Are you sure you're all right?"

He twisted the cold water out of the wash cloth and put it back on Kim's forehead. "I'm okay, I think."

With the contraction gone, Kim sank down onto the pillows and sleepily asked, "Mary, how much longer?"

"Maybe one or two contractions," I remarked. "Your baby's head is ready to be born."

Kim's breathing got heavy again. With her eyes closed and her mouth opened, she pushed and groaned, "Ahhh. Oohhh."

"Kim, take a deep breath and give me one more hard push," I coached. She gave a monumental effort.

"Here comes your baby," I shouted. Within a split second, Gary's hands were on the slippery, crying newborn along with mine. I worked quickly to dry

116

the chubby infant and wrap a warm blanket around him. Gary's face turned red with excitement.

As I cut the cord, Gary exclaimed, "He's mine. He's mine! Here's my boy!"

Kim perked up. "Wait a minute. I did all the work. I get him. He's mine!"

Kim stretched out her hands, only to hear from Gary, "No, no. He's mine." Standing next to me, Gary cradled the baby in his arms.

"No, I want to hold my son," Kim stated emphatically.

"He's mine too," Gary exclaimed.

"He's mine, too," Kim asserted, "Give him to me."

My head bobbed back and forth like a ping pong ball listening to the two of them. I interrupted, "Well, I helped him be born, so I get to hold him." They stared at me in silence. Then we all howled.

Gary handed the baby to Kim, gave her a kiss, and informed us, "Well, he *is* mine!" With a twinkle in his eye he said to Kim, "But I'll let you hold him just for a little while."

Bungee Jumper

Georgia, a home birth midwife, practices in an upper-middle class community in California where life seems picture perfect–usually.

Lily was an interior designer. She would meticulously plan down to the finest detail every single item needed to furnish and decorate a luxurious room. She also knew how to plan each intimate detail for the perfect, most serene, and spiritual home birth.

My nurse, Karen, had met with Lily previously and was clueing me in on her list of requests. "Listen, Georgia," Karen informed me, "a lot of these requests are the usual–slow delivery of the head, avoid an episiotomy if possible, place the baby on her abdomen after delivery, wait to cut the cord, and all that. But there's more."

Karen continued as her right eyebrow lifted in a wry expression, "Lily also requests that conversation be kept to a minimum: whispering only. The drapes will be drawn shut. The only lighting will come from candles placed strategically around the bedroom. Her music CDs are scheduled in a certain order, and her husband will be in charge of the sound system. She plans to burn rare incense that she ordered from China. Are you getting the picture here, Georgia?"

"Got it," I responded, "very clearly!"

A couple weeks later, Karen whispered to me over the phone from Lily's home, "You should see this place. It's gorgeous!" Karen then informed me that Lily's contractions were mild but becoming more regular. Since Lily's first baby came really fast, I decided to head over and beat the five o'clock rush-hour traffic.

I parked my car along the circular, bricked driveway and folded the map to her home. The physician on call and backup hospital were just two blocks away. I reviewed Lily's detailed list of requests one more time. Pulling my black bag of supplies and a full oxygen tank out of the back seat, I thought, "This should be an interesting experience."

The manicured lawn was a deep forest green. Taking a deep breath, the

118

aroma of freshly cut grass filled my lungs. Rose bushes wrapped the pillars that framed the front steps. The chimes of Big Ben echoed after I pressed the doorbell. Through stained glass I saw Karen approach and open the massive door with an amused expression. "Lily's upstairs in the bedroom. Follow me."

We climbed the curved oak stairway, carpeted in white plush, up to the second level. Lily was propped up in bed sipping some herbal tea. Rose petals sat in a silver bowl on her dresser, matching the deep red brocade of her duvet bed cover and curtains. Incense filled the air along with soft, classical music piped in through hidden speakers. Candles were everywhere, playfully flickering warm shadows across the perfect blend of rich paneling and textured walls.

"Hi, Lily. How are you doing?" I asked softly.

"I'm doing well, Georgia. The contractions are getting stronger, but they are not terribly uncomfortable yet." She'd been through this before.

"Where's your little Adam?" I asked quietly.

Lily's husband, Jon, answered as he entered the room, "He's already with Grandma. They're on their way to a movie. Welcome, Georgia. How are you?"

"Just great," I began to answer when Lily grabbed my sleeve.

"Georgia, let's go over my birth plan one more time. You have the list, right?"

"I wouldn't leave home without it," I responded, holding it up for her to see and catching a wink from Jon. We reviewed her requests together.

Jon had a wonderful sense of humor which seemed to balance Lily's oh-so-serious and compulsive personality. He gently teased, "Now, Lily, the midwife has been here five minutes already. Don't you think you should put this list aside and get these contractions rolling, Hon?"

"If it were up to me, this baby would be out and nursing by now, sweetie," she replied through slightly clenched teeth.

"Let's see what progress you're making," I told Lily, breaking the tension.

Her cervix was four centimeters dilated and very soft. The baby's head was low in the pelvis. I informed Lily and Jon, "All we need now are some regular contractions. Once things get going it'll probably be pretty fast, like

119

Adam's birth." Then I added, "The fetal heart beat is good, and Karen will keep checking it. I'm going to make myself a cup of tea in the kitchen, and then I'll be right back up. Just yell if you need anything. And by the way, Lily, it would be good if you could get up and walk. That could be all that's needed to get your labor going."

"Oh, I'm not so sure I'm ready for a walk yet, Georgia," sighed Lily.

Jon caught my eye and gave me a wink. "Five minutes, Lady Lily, and I will escort you up and down the hall."

I found a mug in the kitchen cupboard, filled it with water, and zapped it in the microwave. A wicker basket of tea selections had been set out for me, along with blueberry and raspberry scones. "How lovely," I noted. "There should be plenty of time for a snack." Sitting at the kitchen table was a pleasure that included a view of the flower garden and gazebo in their landscaped backyard.

While I nibbled the rich biscuit, my mind drifted momentarily, but my reverie was suddenly interrupted by a horrendous scream. I ran up to the bedroom, taking two steps at a time. "My water broke! And it's soaking the carpet!" Lily wailed. She was bent over, staring at the puddle that was saturating the carpet when the next contraction hit. Karen and Jon held her arms at each side. "Aauugghh! My baaaaaaaack! I never felt this with Adam!" Lily wasn't whispering.

I silently realized, "This baby's coming so fast my tea will probably still be warm when I get back to the kitchen!"

"Take a breath, Lily. You're doing great! This looks like another fast delivery," I said, trying to prepare Lily for the extra challenge that often occurs with a quick birth–the intense and abrupt physical sensations from the baby moving down so rapidly.

"I'll help you back to bed and get you a pad to catch the fluid," said Karen. As they stopped in the bathroom, Karen started to place a pad on Lily to catch the fluid.

"This is a lost cause," snapped Lily as fluid gushed down her leg and onto the glistening marble floor.

120

"So much for dry socks," said Jon, who smiled as he took his off and tossed them into the bathtub.

Lily ripped off her pad and sat on the toilet. "Another contraction!" she yelled.

"Do you want to get back into bed?" I asked.

"No-o-o-o-o!" grunted Lily. I knew that sound, a low tone that came with the pushing stage.

"Karen, get my delivery kit *now*," I instructed as Lily's face reddened with the irresistible urge to bear down. "The baby's coming. Can you lift her off the toilet, Jon?"

Jon awkwardly lifted Lily under her arms, squatting and bracing himself against the tiled wall. While putting on my gloves, Karen returned with the delivery kit, already open. She grabbed Lily's other arm, trying to relieve Jon of some of the weight. I was on my knees as Lily sank down onto the cold floor.

"The head's coming out. It's coming. It's out, Lily!" The volume of my voice rose abruptly. Then I remembered–Lily wanted it quiet. I promptly switched to a whisper. "And the face is already pink. Now give me a tiny, gentle push, and we'll get those shoulders out." Lily pushed, but it was neither tiny nor gentle. It seemed she pushed with all the energy that had been pent up in her body for the last nine months.

Time momentarily halted and then transcended into slow motion. With this huge effort from Lily, the baby squirted out, followed by another flood of clear amniotic fluid. In fact, the baby's wet skin slid right through my hands, past my knees, and across the slick marble floor. The umbilical cord remained intact, stretching like taffy as the baby flew right by me. At the cord's maximum length, about two feet, the baby's motion miraculously came to a stop. Then the cord recoiled back toward Lily, spinning the baby around like a turtle on its back. The baby started screaming. Karen covered him with a warm blanket as I quickly scooped him up.

"It's another boy!" I exclaimed out loud, but embarrassment consumed me, as I thought to myself, "I can't believe I let that happen!"

121

Looking up at Jon, I immediately knew that eye contact would be a mistake. Jon was laughing madly. "He's just like a greased pig! He's our little bungee jumper, Lily!" Jon again started to hoot and holler and then saw the sober look on Lily's face. This was not quite what she had planned. He swallowed his laughter and tried in vain to hold it in.

"Oh no, don't you start laughing now!" I fearfully cautioned myself, choking down a giggle and clearing my throat to try to cover it up.

"Here's your handsome son," I announced to Lily, trying to maintain my composure and preserve the last shred of sophistication left in the room. But it was a lost cause. The crackle in my voice gave me away. Thank goodness Lily didn't seem to notice as she reached for her new son and held him tightly to her chest. Meanwhile Karen kept her head down as if she was busying herself with the instruments, but I could see her shoulders shaking as she snorted under her breath.

None of us moved from our bathroom positions. Looking up at Jon once again it was clear why he remained motionless behind Lily. Tears were running down his face as it contorted in every which way, as he tried desperately to hold in his emotions. He did not want to ruin this sweet moment for his lovely, but still serious wife.

From then on I avoided all eye contact with Jon, knowing that with one look between us, I'd just lose it. We calmly delivered the placenta and got things cleaned up.

"Oh dear God, please don't let me start laughing or I won't be able to stop!" I prayed repeatedly over the next few hours.

Not until my drive home did I allow myself to let it all out. That first uncontrollable giggle escalated into nonstop sobs of breath-stopping hilarity. I had to pull the car into a parking lot to regain a bit of composure.

I could hardly breathe by the time I walked through the door of my humble little home, an eclectic hodgepodge of treasures from my years of garage sales. My husband looked up from his newspaper, saw my red face and blotchy eyes, and asked, "Oh my goodness, honey, what's wrong?" He immediately got up from his chair and put his arms around me as I once again collapsed into uncontrollable laughter.

For the next ten minutes as he tried to console me, all I could utter was, "We delivered a bungee jumper!"

High Tech, High Touch

Belinda loves to include reluctant fathers-to-be during prenatal visits as well as during the birth process.

Scott liked machines. He sat quietly in my office, engrossed in his state-of-the-art cell phone, not saying a word. I tried to include him in the discussion. He and his wife Cindy were expecting their first child.

"Do you have any questions, Scott?" I tried to make eye contact with him.

He looked up and responded quietly, "No."

Cindy, on the other hand, was very outgoing. Freckles covered her cheeks. She was full of smiles and questions. As we talked, Scott took notes on his cell phone which seemed to be glued to his hand.

"Let's see how this baby is growing." Cindy lay down on the exam table. She lifted her blouse as I stretched the measuring tape from her pubic bone to the top of her uterus. Her abdomen was shaped like a bubble on her slender body. Smiling, I informed them, "Your baby is growing perfectly."

I placed my hands over Cindy's abdomen and checked the baby's position. "Do you want to feel the baby's head, Scott?" I asked, trying again to include him. "It's right here."

"No, that's okay, Belinda," he replied awkwardly. This whole experience was quite different from his computer world. We all listened to the strong, regular beat of the baby's heart.

"What's the rate today?" Scott asked.

"144 beats per minute. Just perfect," I reassured him. He recorded the number in his electronic notepad.

Six months later, with Carol five days overdue, a fetal monitoring test was done to check the baby's heart rate pattern. While placing the soft belt around her circular abdomen, Scott sat in front of the monitor. He studied the paper tracing which documented each individual beat. The pattern looked good, reflecting a healthy baby, and I sent them home to wait for the beginning of labor.

The next day Cindy called, "Belinda, I think my water broke, and I'm starting to have a few contractions."

"Then it's time to come in," I advised. The sun shone into my eyes on my way to the hospital, only five blocks from home.

While preparing the birthing room, I recalled seeing Cindy and Scott on their first prenatal visit. They were unhappy with the prenatal care that they had previously received in their hometown, one hour away. Cindy had shared, "It didn't feel right. The doctor ordered a lot of tests without explaining them to us first, and he didn't spend a lot of time with me." She didn't want any unnecessary interventions performed and felt that the doctor wasn't really listening to her. Despite the longer drive, they decided to have their baby at our rural midwife practice.

I kept this in mind as they arrived at the labor and delivery unit. Cindy's cervix was dilated five centimeters already. Contractions were strong and three minutes apart. Labor was progressing quickly.

"Is everything ok?" Cindy asked between contractions.

"Yes. It's all going very smoothly, and you're doing exceptionally well," I reassured her and then asked, "Would you like to sit in the jacuzzi?" She agreed and settled into the tub for the rest of her labor. Cindy sipped from her glass of juice regularly and changed positions every now and then. She looked comfortable and secure with the soothing water bubbling around her.

Scott set up the video camera and the boom box. I couldn't help but compare the two of them in my mind, thinking, "He also looks secure but in a whole different way–surrounded by his machines." Soft piano music began to drift through the air.

For another two hours, she labored in the tub. I helped Cindy adjust her breathing to accommodate the increasing intensity of the contractions. Suddenly she spoke up. "Belinda! I need to push!" I turned off the jets. Cindy grabbed

125

hold of the side bars and began to push. Scott continued to videotape, watching the events unfold through the lens of his camera.

"Am I doing okay?" Cindy asked.

"You're doing great. With the next contraction, tuck your chin down to your chest and really focus on pushing that baby down and out," I coached her.

After another twenty minutes, the baby's head emerged. Together Cindy and I lifted the baby out and onto her chest. Cindy's proud glow covered her face. The baby let out a cry and snuggled under her chin. Their new daughter, Samantha, was pink and healthy.

Scott cautiously walked out from behind the video camera and looked with his own eyes, from his wife to his child. "Oh, look at her fingernails! Look at her hair! Isn't she gorgeous!" he exclaimed with awe.

Cindy chose to stay the full two days on the maternity unit to have extra help with breastfeeding. Monday arrived and I was working on paperwork in my office. There was a knock on the door. It was a surprise to see the new family standing there like deer in the headlights, frozen with fear. They spoke in very serious tones and whispered, "We don't want to go home, Belinda. We're scared." Cindy's eyes filled with tears.

I paused, thinking, "No one has ever said this to me before." Scott looked totally lost. No amount of technology could prepare him for the realities of fatherhood.

Ushering them into a private consultation room, we talked it all through, including specific instructions for mom, dad, and baby. I particularly encouraged Cindy to get enough rest, drink plenty of fluids, and call if any danger signs occurred.

"You're going to do great," I reassured them. "Call us with anything at all. We have a public health nurse coming to your home tomorrow, so you won't be alone. And Scott, here's some information just for you." I handed him a packet of brochures for new fathers. "Let's go over some things that you can do to help."

Two weeks later, Scott and Cindy returned for a postpartum visit. Cindy chatted nonstop. While cuddling Samantha, she described in detail their success

126

with breastfeeding. Amazingly, Scott did not stop talking either. He conversed on and on about Samantha's schedule, her habits, her expressions and accomplishments. Not once did he refer to his electronic notes. Scott was beaming. "Belinda, look at what she can do!" he exclaimed. He gently lifted Samantha from Cindy's arms and showed how she could already hold her head upright.

A new family was born. Scott's hands were fully occupied, but no longer with his high tech gizmos. Instead they were replaced by his living, breathing, cuddly daughter.

Can't Sit Still

Ruth is a veteran midwife who sits with hundreds of laboring women in this 50-bed rural hospital. She is, however, acutely aware that sitting is not necessarily a requirement for birth.

Sarah was in constant motion. She jumped out of bed with a vengeance after having her cervix examined. It was dilated five centimeters, and Sarah was in active labor. The peach bedspread fell to the floor. As the next contraction began, I encouraged her to lean forward onto her husband, Bill. "Oh, you're too bony!" she told him. She rushed up to me before the contraction got any stronger. "Oh, Ruth, you're too soft."

Sarah then ran to the bathroom door adjoining the birthing room. She grabbed the knobs on each side of the door, tightened her grip, and pressed her head forward into the hard wood. Unlike the rhythmic breathing that is taught in childbirth classes, Sarah's breaths were irregular and off-beat. The contraction peak caught her off guard and she let out a loud throaty groan. This was followed by a few quick pants in and out. When the contraction ended, she exhaled loudly and walked nonstop around the room, searching for the ideal position for her next contraction.

The nurse, Kathy, and I followed her with the fetal monitor. Luckily it was on wheels. Kathy lifted her hospital gown while I quickly placed the round monitor "toco" onto her lower abdomen. Years of ballet had sculpted her slender, petite, and very muscular body. The tracing of the fetal heart beat showed the baby was tolerating labor just fine. "Sounds terrific!" I reassured us all.

Sarah suddenly shooed us away and blew right by me. She leaned on the counter as the next contraction started. Shaking her head in frustration, Sarah ran back to the bathroom door.

Bill stood close by, not reaching for her, but there for her to reach. He did not even try to coach her, but wisely sensed that she was following her own instincts, doing her own thing. He remained calm and quiet. In fact, the whole

128

room was silent except for the low guttural sounds erupting from deep within Sarah's soul.

I gently touched the "on" button of the radio to provide some soft, calming background music. "It's too much!" Sarah snapped. "Turn it off, Ruth. It's distracting!" I promptly complied.

Someone watching this scenario might think Sarah was absolutely wired and her behavior totally outlandish. Although her eyes were wide with intensity, she was not in distress. Others might have wondered if there was a real problem, but Bill, Kathy, and I knew otherwise. Although Sarah's behavior was out of the ordinary, even for us, we could see that she was tuned in to her body. She trusted the messages she was receiving and was driven by each moment of every single labor sensation.

"Would you like to try the rocking chair?" I asked.

She sat down and started to rock back and forth, then hopped right out of it. "Augh! It just doesn't feel right," she reported with the next contraction.

Sarah moved quickly, her fuzzy pink slippers sliding across the linoleum floor as if she were skating. Then, without any warning, she plunked right down on the floor and roared, "A-A-U-U-G-H!"

Kathy and I rushed to her side. She let out a piercing cry as an enormous urge to push overtook her. There was a splash of clear water on the floor. I knew the baby was not far behind. Sarah's eyes shut tightly as she pushed again and again.

Kathy positioned the delivery cart behind me and opened the sterile pack of instruments. I slipped on my gloves. After the next contraction, Bill and I each took an arm and lifted Sarah onto the bed. Her labia separated to reveal a circle of sandy colored hair. The area expanded within seconds, stretching the smooth perineum around it. Reaching for the bulb syringe, I noticed Kathy's eyes widen. We both watched this circle continue to enlarge and then grow even further. It felt as if we were suddenly in slow motion.

The huge round head emerged, and the baby squeezed out of Sarah's tiny, sleek body. Sarah let out a scream of pure relief and joy. Tears ran down her face

129

and Bill's eyes filled with emotion as they embraced their new daughter. Kathy and I paused in absolute astonishment at what we had just witnessed. I could hardly wait to place the baby on the scale–nine pounds, twelve ounces!

Later, after signing the birth certificate and completing my paperwork, I stopped in to check on Sarah. She was settled into her maternity room, holding her new daughter. Sarah saw me enter and immediately looked down at the baby.

"I am so embarrassed!" she confessed. "I behaved terribly in labor. Ruth, I'm so ashamed." She then returned my gaze, as if searching my eyes for a response.

"That's just not true!" I answered firmly, without any hesitation. "You were absolutely beautiful. You listened to your body, to all of your natural instincts, and you did everything you needed to do to deliver this baby. You showed remarkable strength. And, to top it off, you had a *huge* baby! Kathy and I will never forget what we witnessed you do."

As a midwife, I've watched hundreds of women listen to their bodies and trust their instincts. A natural power emerges. Then there's Sarah, who went through this process with a unique and extraordinary intensity, determination, and strength. And yet she was feeling embarrassed. I hoped my words were helping Sarah to be proud of how she had labored and given birth. If she continued to follow her instincts, those same innate powers would carry her through motherhood.

Sarah remained uncharacteristically still. A look of realization slowly came across her face and her eyes met mine. "I *did* do good, didn't I," Sarah agreed. She laid her head back on the pillow and grinned with delight, instinctively cuddling her baby. And this time, she stayed in bed.

Neat 'n Clean

Laura, a recent graduate, uses her midwifery skills during an African experience, and in particular those involving sterile technique.

"Quick Miss Laura, get your delivery apron on," Yolanda urged me in her staff sergeant voice. She was standing at the side window of the maternity hut. I followed her gaze and saw a woman squatting behind a low bush, but didn't think much about it. I ignored her order and continued my survey of this brand new environment.

It was my first day in Nigeria. Yolanda was finishing a tour of the facilities that would be my home for the next two years. She had just explained that the large hut served as a dorm to house women who had high-risk pregnancies. During their eighth month, these women came from all over the country, up to two hundred miles away, to await the births of their babies. This dorm became their home away from home. When the women went into labor, they were taken up to the hospital for their delivery. If, however, there was an emergency, gloves and an apron were kept on a shelf in the hut.

"Put your delivery apron on!" Yolanda yelled at me again.

Her voice jolted me out of my trance. A puzzled look appeared on my face as I wondered, "Me? Now? What is she talking about?" Yolanda might have been speaking Swahili.

Yolanda pointed to the woman behind the bush and spelled it out for me. "She's having her baby. You'd better get your apron and gloves on."

My eyes widened and my mouth dropped open as I looked more carefully at the woman squatting over a scooped out hole in the ground–the hole that served as their toilet facility.

"Oh my gosh!" I cried, horrified. "She can't do that! She's not in the hospital!"

131

Inside my newly trained midwife mind I was screaming, "What about the equipment, the delivery table with sterile drapes, the antiseptic solution for washing?"

Yolanda, with one hand on her hip, eyeballed me and pointed her finger once more. "Miss Laura, if you don't hurry, she's going to have that baby without you!"

I ran outside and shouted to the woman, "Don't push yet! I have to get my gloves and sterile instruments!"

The puzzled look from the squatting mother told me she didn't understand a word of English.

I rolled my eyes and shook my head, "This must be the culture shock the mission experts talked about." I wanted to cry, but held back tears as my fantasy of a pristine "first delivery" in this unfamiliar country fell to pieces.

The woman's groan called me back to reality. Her puffed face and set jaw told me that I had better hurry. I raced back to the maternity hut for emergency supplies. The apron was hanging on a hook and a pair of rubber gloves rested on the shelf. That's all there was. There were no long sleeved cover gowns, no masks, no goggles, and no sterile equipment.

While scurrying back to the woman, I pulled the plastic apron over my head, but it was too long for me. I tripped and landed face down in the dirt. Keeping my hands high while holding the precious gloves, I thought, "At least they're still clean." Picking myself up, I put on the first glove and then the second as I ran to the woman and knelt beside her.

"Ok, I'm ready any time you are," I informed the woman and nodded, while forcing down a giggle. "God only knows what my prim and proper instructors would say if they could see me now!"

My eyes widened with a sudden realization that I could catch something more than a baby from the pit below. I moved to the front of the woman, extended my hand toward her vaginal opening, and shook my head, "Don't push just yet." There I was again, giving instructions in English.

132

As I straddled the primitive toilet, the woman remained oblivious to all of my movements and chatter. "Okay, now I'm ready." I smiled and nodded encouragement. But my thoughts challenged me. "I can't believe this is happening. It's not supposed to be like this."

I looked over my shoulder and shouted to Yolanda, "Please get the fetascope so I can listen to the baby's heartbeat. Also bring some hot water and towels. And hurry." Yolanda meandered slowly back to the medical area, taking one deliberate step at a time. I realized this had the makings of a disaster. There probably wasn't even time to check the fetal heart rate. Not with these strong pushes.

A crowd of pregnant women gathered at the doorway of the hut. Their big brown eyes were fixed on me. What a time for them to check out the new midwife! I scolded myself for getting a little unnerved. "Calm down and get your act together." I took a breath, "What was I thinking when I agreed to do this for two full years?" More questions arose. "What past pregnancy complication brought this woman here for her birth? Was it a stillbirth or a cesarean section? Where's the chart?" Advice to myself then followed. "Don't even go there, Laura. It'll just make you more anxious."

The woman's grunts were louder now. I inhaled and exhaled deeply to help myself relax, then secretly wished for a face mask. The stench from the hole forced me to move to her side. Pressing my nose into my shoulder, I kept one eye on her perineum. It was amazing to see the young woman so focused on the work she needed to do.

I quickly looked for Yolanda, but she had not yet emerged from the hut. In my head, my teacher's words came back to me: "You can do this. Be creative. Remember the basics." This was followed by a quick prayer. "God, make this turn out all right, and please, please get Yolanda here fast!"

With the next push, the baby's head began to emerge. I took another frantic look around for Yolanda and murmured another urgent prayer. "God, please don't let me drop this newborn into the pit."

133

By the end of the push, the head was delivered. The mother readjusted her feet and gave a final push for the shoulders. The newborn boy's sleek body filled my hands as the warm amniotic fluid gushed out and into the hole. My arms were shaking. The infant's cry brought clapping and cheers from the spectators. Fearful of dropping the baby, I quickly brought him up to his mom's arms as she sat back on the ground. One of the pregnant women offered me her shawl, and I used it to dry and wrap the baby.

A gentle tap on my shoulder surprised me. There was Yolanda smiling broadly, as if I had just passed a test. She handed me a cord clamp and scissors. After cutting the cord I asked, "Well, Yolanda, what next?"

"Just wait for the placenta, Miss Laura," she instructed. "As it delivers, remove the clamp and let the placenta fall into the hole. That way, everything will be neat 'n clean."

Her response caught me off guard. I chuckled and replied, "Yeah, right. Neat 'n clean."

Dolly, I'm Not!

Lynda, an experienced midwife, is not particularly well-endowed. She provides well women health care in a suburban office in the northern U.S.

I would never be mistaken for Dolly Parton. And, I noticed, neither would my patient Rita who was here for her annual exam. I listened to her heart and lungs with my stethoscope as she lay on the exam table.

"Your lungs are clear, and your heart sounds great, Rita," I remarked. "Your breast exam is next. Let's start by having you place your arms above your head like this." As her slender arms rose upwards, I explained, "This position stretches out the breast tissue and allows me to do a better exam."

As part of my routine, I further explained to Rita a few important tips on how to do self-breast exams at home. "Get to know how they look and feel now. That way, if there are any changes down the road, you'll pick them up right away. It may be a lump or simply a toughening of the tissue. Or, if you look in the mirror and see a pulling or dimpling of the breasts that wasn't there before, be sure to come in and get it checked out." I added with a smile, "And please tell your husband to let you know if he notices any changes. Partners have picked up a significant number of breast lumps. Truly!" Rita chuckled.

Proceeding with the exam, I could easily feel each rib on her chest, covered by a very thin layer of breast tissue. "Kind of like mine," I thought to myself.

"By the way, how old are you?" I asked.

"I'll be forty-two next month," Rita replied.

"Have you ever had a mammogram?" I questioned.

She hesitated, looking down at her slim chest, then answered, "No, not yet."

I checked her second breast and began to explain the value of having a baseline mammogram. Rita quickly glanced up at me as her eyes paused for a split second at my chest. Her eyebrows rose, and a quizzical look came across her

135

face.

I chuckled inside and immediately stopped my exam. "I know exactly what you're thinking." I pointed to my breasts, exclaiming, "Yes, Rita, they even managed to get these babies into that mammogram machine!" We simultaneously burst into laughter realizing our breasts *could* successfully be mammogrammed, even though Dolly *we're not.*

Ask the Expert

Sharon brings her youngest son with her when she moves from the Midwest to the coast to complete her midwifery education. He receives quite an education as well.

My youngest son Matt had always been the shyest of my three boys. When I decided to move to the east coast to complete my master's degree in midwifery, Matt agreed to come with me. At fourteen years old, he decided to leave our small Illinois town for this two-year adventure. Matt's courage surprised me. This change would mean leaving his friends, older brothers, and soccer team during his first two years of high school.

Matt and I both experienced the challenges of a new beginning. As I readjusted to life from a working Mom to a university student, Matt tried to navigate his east coast high school. My quiet, reserved son struggled as a freshman. He tried making friends, but had trouble breaking into the established cliques. Eventually, Matt decided to quit the soccer team. I could see his loneliness growing. Each day his shoulders slumped a little more. His smile drooped down at the edges.

Yet every day after school, he raced up the stairs to read in his arched window nook, a favorite spot that seemed to provide some security. Engrossed in my own studies, however, I had no idea what he was reading. I assumed it was homework or maybe some books from the library and didn't give it much thought.

One morning, as I skimmed through one of my midwifery textbooks during breakfast, a purple and gold bookmark slipped from the page. My eyebrows furrowed in confusion as it fluttered to the floor. It was Matt's bookmark with his favorite football team's logo printed on it. I looked up to see my son blushing as he stood in the kitchen doorway.

While I had assumed he was reading teen fiction, he had been turning the pages of my midwifery books. Matt had also read *Our Bodies, Our Selves* from cover to cover. He had even studied the detailed medical text of *William's Obstetrics*. "All you had to do was ask for a library card, you poor kid!" I teased.

After our first year away from the Midwest, Matt asked to move back home. It took me only two seconds to agree, knowing how lonely he'd been. I sent him back to live with my oldest son, Jack, and his wife, while I finished my midwifery education. It was clearly the right decision. Back in our small town with his childhood friends, Matt returned to his happy self.

Fall arrived and with it a new school year. I was at peace with Matt moving back home and could focus on my studies without worrying about his loneliness. However, one day in late September, I received a phone call from his high school. Matt had gotten into some trouble. The principal, an old friend of mine, informed me, "Sharon, you've got yourself a smart-ass kid who thinks he knows more about women's health than the teacher."

Confused, I asked for more information. The principal explained that Matt had challenged his teacher about a specific women's health topic, and he had refused to back down. Out of frustration, the teacher ordered Matt to teach a class on women's health the next day.

"Well, let him teach it then!" I replied.

The next evening Jack reported back to me, "Mom, you would have been so proud. Matt conducted himself like the main speaker at a clinical seminar! The health teacher and the principal couldn't believe how well he answered all of the students' questions. Their faces showed a new shade of red today."

Jack shared more details. During the class, Matt had instructed his classmates to write down any health question or concern they had on a piece of paper. The anonymous notes were then passed to him. He read each one aloud with professionalism and answered them with clarity.

One of the girls in the class had asked, "When you put a tampon in, can you lose it?"

Matt had calmly replied, "No, you've just misplaced it. There's no place for it to go. Let me show you on this poster of the female body."

138

This first inquiry started a deluge of questions that continued to the end of class. Matt answered every question, even questions that the teacher had been too embarrassed to address.

Later that day, I received a follow-up call from the principal, still glowing red from Matt's presentation. "Sharon, where the heck did he learn all this?"

I proudly answered, "In midwifery school!"

Chapter 5: Life Complications

Perfectly laid plans and expectations can be shattered by a single complication, in a single, split-second moment. Lessons learned from one's response to a complication can be as significant as the event itself.

Come Right In

Vicky, a graduate nurse-midwife, faces a difficult decision after hearing the results of her national board exam. This leads her on a retreat to the Badlands of South Dakota.

"Come right in," Cindy, my midwife, told me. Those three words, along with the concern in her beckoning voice, were exactly what I needed to hear. Behind the closed door of the exam room, she listened to my story again. I explained how my body was burning with a fever and aching all over. I felt very alone caring for my three-week-old daughter, Amelia. My family was all up north. I didn't like being a transplant in the big state of Texas, where my husband was stationed. There was no one here to help me, even if I could overcome my stubborn independence enough to admit that I needed a hand.

Cindy knew me well. Less than a month ago, she spent an endless night helping me through the labor and birth of my daughter. I would always remember her calming affirmations. "You're strong. You'll get through this. You will be a good mom. You can do this." Even during prenatal visits Cindy always listened, acknowledged my fears, and eased my mind. I knew she would once again take care of me.

"Come right in." Those three reassuring words would echo throughout my life, eventually leading me down a path to a new career.

Many years passed since my encounter with Cindy, but I never forgot how she treated me. She inspired me to become a nurse after the birth of my son. My nursing career led me to the pediatric intensive care unit. I loved the challenge that came with intensive care, but I wanted to do more and craved greater independence.

Looking back at my first pregnancy and birth experience, I wanted to be handing healthy babies to their mothers instead of handling critically ill children. A special grant opened the doors to a midwifery education. Following the board exams, I was welcomed into an established nurse-midwife practice. What more

142

could a new graduate ask than to be surrounded by caring, experienced midwives while waiting for those all-important exam results?

"Come right in," said Peggy, my midwife director. I slowly entered and she closed the door. Passing the certification exam had eluded me for the third time by a mere two points. I was at rock bottom. We both knew that I could no longer practice midwifery because of these results, but I was not prepared for what she had to say next. "I want you to retake the exam. But this time, you need to attend the refresher course before the test. I'll even use our continuing education money to pay for it."

As I stared at her in disbelief, tears filled my eyes. I had already done everything in my power to prepare for that exam. After three failures, I didn't think I could handle another disappointment, and exclaimed. "I can't. I just can't."

Peggy immediately countered, "You can if you want to! I know you can pass. I've worked with you and have seen for myself. You are a good midwife. You can't give up your dream. You'll get through this. You're strong. I'm asking you to try one more time."

She sounded exactly like the midwife I knew her to be. Those familiar words resonated in my body. Structured exams had always stymied me. I had been willing to try again in the past, but this time Peggy's request overwhelmed me. I was ready to scream for an educational epidural to end the pain, ready to admit failure and give up my dream career.

The situation forced me to wonder, "Why have so many doors opened to get me to this point only to slam shut in my face now?" Failing again would be a real blow. I looked at Peggy, her eyes shining with confidence. She was not taking no for an answer. I sighed and nodded my head, but quickly added, "I need time to think and pray about this."

"That's a deal," she said, shaking my hand firmly.

I chose to contemplate my career over a four-day retreat near the Badlands of South Dakota. I asked God, "Since you apparently don't want me to be a midwife, what exactly do you want me to do with my life?"

143

After getting settled into my room at the Jesuit retreat house, I took a short drive to a trailhead to begin a solitary and meditative hike in the Badlands. The residents of South Dakota viewed the area as beautiful, but they named the area "Badlands" for good reason. The terrain was mountainous and every turn looked the same. It was easy to get lost if you didn't stay on the marked trails. I carefully checked the posted maps along the way while spending the day hiking and journaling.

Before returning to the retreat house late afternoon, I wanted one more strenuous hike. One of the park rangers suggested a short but challenging path. He assured me the trail was well marked and my hiking boots would be added security for the rocky surface. Because of the warm temperatures, I peeled off my sweatshirt and tossed it in the car.

It was five thirty in the evening when I reached the halfway point, just as the ranger had described. I carefully climbed the many rungs of a rope ladder 150 feet up a mountain and descended to the other side. I continued my hike to the parking lot but ended up right back at the same rope ladder. I was puzzled, thinking I must have missed a marker. Climbing the ladder again and scaling down the other side, I tried a different path but wound up at the ladder a third time. My anxiety level rose during this next attempt. Up I went over the mountain and down the other side. I carefully checked the signs and hoped to finally see the ranger station and my car, but landed once again at the ladder. At that moment I became truly scared. Darkness was closing in, and I felt the chill of the night–a blast of arctic air.

I sat on a rock and used my cell phone to call for help but heard only static. I tried again. Still static. I climbed back up the ladder to the top of the hill and tried another time. Only static. An intuitive voice encouraged me to take another crack at it. This time I leaned over a cliff and dialed 911.

A man answered, "911 Operator."

"Oh, thank goodness," I exclaimed, "I need help. I'm lost in the Black Hills. No, I mean I'm lost in the Badlands, and can't find my way out." My voice escalated, "Please help me."

144

"Okay, Ma'am, just take it easy and give me some details about where you are," he instructed. I described my location by identifying the highway routes nearby. One mountain looked just like another against the black sky of night. The operator assured me, "I'm going to call the highway patrol, and they will contact the park rangers. They'll find you, but it might take a while."

The operator explained that he was located more than 75 miles from where I was and placed me on hold. Questions raced through my mind while waiting for him to come back on the line. What if I hadn't been able to reach someone? Freezing to death was a chilling thought. It made me shiver. They hadn't found me yet. What if I didn't make it out alive? What would my daughter and son do? Would they be able to find me? Why didn't I bring my sweatshirt? As the cold wind rushed across my bare skin, I started to cry.

Just then the operator came back on the phone. "How are you doing?" he asked.

I burst out sobbing, "I feel panicked!" The operator asked my name. "Vicky," I answered.

He instructed, "Vicky, take a slow, deep breath in. Now, let it out slowly. Stay focused." I pulled the phone from my ear and stared at it in amazement. If I didn't know better, I'd say he had a little midwifery in him.

He asked about my family. "Well," I shared, "my daughter Amelia is engaged to be married next September and just landed her first teaching job for the fall. My son Jonas is studying business law in Michigan." My voice quivered, "My mom is retired. She lives back east. Mom is diabetic. My sisters depend on me to help her."

During this conversation, I realized my phone battery was getting low. After telling the operator, he insisted I hang up to preserve the charge.

"What's your cell phone number?" he asked.

My heart skipped a beat, "It's a new phone. I don't know the number."

He asked, "Can you write down my phone number? If no one comes in thirty minutes, call me back."

145

"All right," I said hesitantly, flipping open my journal to scribble the numbers. It was almost totally dark. How was I going to see this number to call him back? Cold boulders, deep crevices, and hidden canyons surrounded me. One wrong move could lead to a fall, and they would never find me. Images of the 300-foot drop-off and the bridge below filled my mind. Chilled to the bone, I huddled down next to a rock, trying to stay warm and safe.

Within a few minutes, I saw headlights from a vehicle in the distance moving toward me in the pitch blackness. As the jeep got closer, I started to cry again. "Crying won't help them find you," I told myself, choking down my emotion. I called out in a quivering voice, "I'm up here! Here I am." They heard me and shouted back. I yelled louder with tears streaming down my face. They positioned a lady ranger below. She kept me talking. The other four rangers hurried to get the necessary equipment for my rescue. "This isn't going to be on the ten o'clock news, is it?" I asked her.

"No, only if we have to use a helicopter to rescue you," she calmly explained.

"Do I need to worry about animals?" I asked.

"Well, the rattlesnakes aren't out right now," she calmly informed me.

"Thanks," I replied, "that was a little more information than I needed."

The ranger yelled up to me, "I just received a message on the radio. They are on their way up." Shivering in the cold and unable to move, it felt like it would take hours for them to reach me.

Soon I heard footsteps and saw flashlights. I had never been so happy to see strangers in my life and wanted to hug them all. "Are you hurt?" one asked.

"No, no just-t-t-t c-c-c-cold," I stuttered with chattering teeth. Immediately, a ranger took off his jacket and put it over my shoulders. They handed me a flashlight, put me between them, and we made our way down the mountain. My legs were stiff and my toes were numb. We came out at the same spot where I had parked my car. Even in the darkness, they knew where to go. I quickly put on my sweatshirt and coat, asking, "How c-c-c-can I ever th-th-thank you all?"

146

"It's our job," one of them said, and then added, "Um, there is one thing you could do for us, though. Learn your cell phone number."

"I'll do that. Promise."

After settling into my car, I turned on the heat full blast. Returning to the retreat house, I bundled under extra covers and fell into a deep sleep. Questions haunted my dreams that night, circling and spinning out of control. Why did this happen? What does it mean? I replayed the experience over and over in my mind. The next day, while sitting in the amphitheater at Mount Rushmore and writing in my journal, I longed to make sense out of the previous day's experience. Nothing came to me.

Driving home the following day, it finally hit me. I needed to take the midwife exam again. Then a second realization quickly became apparent. Just as I needed help from others when I was lost in the Badlands, I needed to ask for help from my midwife partners. That might be easy for some people to do, but not so for a stubborn, independent person like myself. For me, this was a huge challenge. My strong-willed spirit softened just a bit. "Okay God, I hear you."

Just as I had done on the mountaintop, I asked for help, and help, indeed, was provided. The midwife practice paid the fee for the exam. Another midwife gave me her frequent flyer miles to cover plane fare that allowed me to attend a three-day review class. An instructor reviewed the entire course content with me. My director promised not to fill my staff position until I received the next exam results. My associates generously took extra call shifts to cover my absence.

I retook the midwife exam at the end of June, and we waited. All of us waited. During this time on hold, I realized how extremely blessed I was, surrounded by friends who believed in me. They generously opened the door for me to discover the courage to ask for help, and they graciously gave it.

In early August, there was a knock on my door. The postman handed me a certified letter. "You'll need to sign for this."

Without thinking, I responded, "Come right in." There were those three words again!

With shaking hands, I tore open the envelope. Pulling out the letter, slowly unfolding it, and scanning the first line, I read: "We are pleased to inform you that you have passed your Board Exam." I closed my eyes, held the letter to my chest, and screamed, *"I'm in!"*

Not So Simple

Nicole routinely provides comprehensive physical exams to women of all ages in this generally healthy, affluent community and usually obtains routine results.

"I'm just here for my yearly pap," Tracey told me.

It sounded simple to me. "Okay Tracey. Let's start by reviewing your health history."

Tracey was a healthy, 26-year-old woman, college-educated, and very self-confident. She was happily married and denied any history of abuse. Her menstrual periods were normal and regular, without any cramping. She was a nonsmoker. Tracey had no medical problems or significant family history. She had no history of major surgeries or illnesses. Tracey had never been pregnant and took the birth control pill correctly at the same time each day. There was no drug or alcohol use in Tracey's history. She exercised five times per week. When asked, Tracey had no questions or concerns at all.

"This is *really* simple," I thought to myself, "This young woman does everything right."

"I'll step out while you change into this gown," I explained. "Then we'll get your physical and pap done."

I returned to the room with a stethoscope around my neck. Tracey sat with excellent posture on the exam table. I placed my hands at her neck area and routinely checked her thyroid and lymph nodes.

Lifting the stethoscope from around my neck and then, before placing it on her upper back, I warned, "This might be cold." My instructions followed. "Take some deep breaths in and out." I listened closely and then asked Tracey to lie back as I placed the stethoscope on her chest.

"Your lungs sound very healthy. You can breathe normally again. I'm going to listen to your heart now." I expected to hear the typical thud–thud, thud–thud, thud–thud in this fit young woman. Instead, there were some significant pauses between each beat. I couldn't believe what I was hearing. My stethoscope

149

remained on her chest longer than usual. Tracey glanced up with a questioning look in her eyes.

"I'm hearing an unusual rhythm, Tracey," I informed her, and then asked, "Have you ever been told that you have an irregular heart beat?"

Tracey responded rather nonchalantly, "I might have been told there was a little irregularity a year or so ago, but nothing major."

"How much caffeine do you drink? Soft drinks, tea, or coffee?" I inquired, searching for a reason for this uncommon finding.

"None," she replied. She denied ever experiencing any unusual cardiac symptoms such as chest pain or shortness of breath. We reviewed her medical and family history again. There were no clues as to why her heart beat would be so irregular.

Tracey asked, "What does this mean? What causes this? Is it serious?"

"Honestly, I have no idea why this is happening," I answered, and further explained, "You have absolutely no risk factors. You have the perfect diet. You exercise regularly. You don't smoke, drink alcohol, or use drugs. You don't even drink caffeine. You do everything right."

Looking directly at Tracey, I continued, "I would feel more comfortable if you got an electrocardiogram–an EKG–here in the lab today. It only takes a few minutes. I'll have a physician review the results before you go home."

Her eyes widened slightly, but she agreed. I completed her physical and pap and gave her the order form to take to the lab. Tracey hesitated and then took the form, realizing that this was not quite the quick in-and-out visit she had planned on. She checked her watch while walking down the hall to the lab.

After seeing the next patient, I returned to my desk. Tracey's EKG results were already clipped to the front of her chart. Tracey returned to the exam room and waited for me to consult with the physician. In the office next to mine, Dr. Brown, an internal medicine specialist, listened as I reviewed Tracey's history. She examined the EKG tracing. Her eyebrows furrowed deeper the longer she looked at it. "I don't know what to make of this," she stated. "Let's send her to Cardiology."

Dr. Brown joined me as we entered the exam room. Together we explained to Tracey that she needed to be seen by a cardiologist as soon as possible. Hearing this news, Tracey's eyes glazed over with confusion and anxiety. Dr. Brown reviewed the test results with her in detail, emphasizing that we didn't yet understand the cause of the findings. After some discussion, Tracey agreed with our plan for a specialist follow-up and had no further questions. I gave her the referral form, which she grasped tightly.

There are some patients who might be too scared to schedule this visit. There are others who might come up with excuses for why this can't fit into their schedule right now. But Tracey, even though she had never faced anything like this before, walked directly to the referral office and left with the appointment card in her hand.

A month later, I received a report from Cardiology with Tracey's name at the top. Listed under "Procedures" was "Implantable Cardiac Cardioverter Defibrillator." I quickly scanned the letter to better understand the medical condition that was diagnosed.

Tracey had a heart condition that could be instantly fatal. As I read on, it became clear: This implant can save her life. I ran the letter to Dr. Brown and shared the news with her.

One year later, I entered an exam room to find Tracey as poised and fit as ever. "Am I ever glad to see you!" I exclaimed.

Tracey shared that when she arrived at Cardiology with our referral a year ago, the nurse had asked abruptly, "What the heck are you doing here?" Tracey didn't look anything like the typical cardiac patients they were used to seeing.

She laughed and further described, "When the specialist listened to my heart, suddenly everyone in the office became so very serious!"

Tracey showed me the implantable defibrillator, placed under her skin at her upper left chest. My fingertips touched the area where the rectangular shaped box sat just below her collar bone. I was awed by the technology that kept Tracey alive.

"You have no idea how happy I am to see you sitting here, alive and

151

healthy, knowing that you're going to be okay," I confided, and couldn't stop beaming.

"I can't thank you enough for discovering the irregular heart beat," Tracey responded.

"All I did was take the time to listen," I explained. "Anyone could have heard this unusual rhythm. You couldn't miss it. But it was you who got yourself to Cardiology. You need to thank yourself for that!" Tracey nodded in appreciation.

"Now what brings you here today?" I asked.

"Just an annual exam." She grinned.

"Sounds simple," I teased. "Let's try to keep it that way!"

Permission Granted

In her thriving Arizona practice, Jill sees many mothers who work outside the home. There are times her role means giving them permission to get balance back into their lives.

Leah's posture said it all. She leaned on her right buttock with her left leg crossed tightly over the right knee. Her shoulders pressed up around her neck. Leah's eyes were closed and her head rested in her hand, supported by her elbow, practically denting the wooden desk. Leah's jaw was clenched. She was alone.

"Mark must be at home with the kids," I thought to myself, and then wondered, "How the heck did she drive here all by herself?"

The dictated report from her postpartum checkup ten days ago detailed a minor problem following Leah's vaginal delivery. There was a small area of wound separation at the site of her stitches. She was back in the clinic sooner than expected, obviously in pain.

I asked softly, "Leah what's wrong?" My question was met with a flood of tears and disconnected words.

Sobbing, she tried to explain, "I think. Oh, I think. I don't know. Wait. Yes, I think I might've pulled my stitches open last night when I sneezed real hard. This was not supposed to happen. It hurts terribly. It burns. I can't take the pain. My kids need me. Why is this happening?" Exhaling deeply, she pleaded, "Please help me!"

"Let's get this checked out right now, Leah, and then we'll see what kind of help you need," I stated confidently. Handing her an exam drape, I instructed, "Once you undress from the waist down, I'll be right in to help you up to the exam table."

The exam confirmed our suspicion. Another stitch was broken at the episiotomy site leaving a gaping wound. The open tissue looked red and raw.

"No wonder you're in pain, Leah," I said, explaining the situation.

"Leah, you said earlier that your kids need you. Is that right?" I questioned gently.

"Well, of course," she affirmed, looking perplexed.

"Okay then, I'm going to put on my director's hat and tell you what I want you to do precisely because your children need you." I prompted, "They need you healthy, don't they?"

"Yes," she acknowledged with a puzzled look.

Then came my challenge. "All right then. Mark must stay home from work today and tomorrow. I want you to ask friends, neighbors, and relatives to come and help you every day for a full week. Here's why," I continued. "In order to heal this wound, you must take a fifteen-minute tub bath three times a day for the entire seven days. Then you need to rest the remaining hours you are awake. And resting means lying on your side in bed or on the couch. The only thing I want you to do is take care of yourself and nurse your baby. Nothing else! Do you understand?"

Leah objected, "That's impossible. I can't. I have two other children."

My response was prompt. "Yes, you can! And furthermore, I mean what I say. Rest means no cooking, cleaning, doing laundry, playing, or running to the store for groceries."

Leah continued to object and blurted out, "But I can't ask for help."

"Yes. Yes, you can. You must. Let me get on my soapbox. Leah, you are the only mother these children will ever have. You love them. Do this for them. You have my permission to take care of yourself. You can't be a good mother if you aren't healthy." I paused, and then kept up my little barrage. "Look at it this way. There are times in our lives when we have the opportunity to give, and there are times when we must be on the receiving end. This is your time to receive." I quieted my voice. "Receive graciously."

I added one last point. "Leah, this is a temporary situation. You will be healed in seven to ten days. Then you can give again."

Leah sat quietly for several seconds. With tears in her eyes she responded, "I guess you're right. It's just difficult for me to ask for help."

154

"That's understandable. It's hard for many of us to switch to the receiving role." As Leah stood to leave, I asked again, "You agree with my plan?"

With a smile she replied, "Yes. Got it."

"Please come back in ten days for a follow-up appointment. If you have a temperature over 100.4 or have more pain than you are having now, I expect a call."

"Yes, Ma'am." She saluted.

Leah returned in ten days. This time she sat erect in the chair, smiling. The dark circles were gone. "Well, how is it going?" I inquired.

"I'm all healed up," Leah replied confidently. A quick exam confirmed Leah's statement.

This time I saluted her. "Congratulations. You can return to mom duty. I officially declare you fully recovered and healthy again."

"There's one more thing," Leah explained, "I've had a lot of time to think. Thank you for giving me permission to take care of myself and to ask others for help. I found out that my friends and family were happy to assist me, and I learned what it means to receive graciously. It was a lesson I needed to learn. Thank you, Jill."

"You're so very welcome," I replied graciously.

Coincidental Intuition

Dana, a veteran midwife, delivers babies in both a birth center and in a near-by hospital on the west coast. No matter what the setting, she regularly witnesses the amazing power of women's intuition.

Lisa asked the question all parents ask right after the birth of their children: "What is it?" Then she asked again, "Is it a boy or girl?" Even though she could hear the baby crying, her questions went unanswered. Both the physician, who delivered the baby by forceps, and the midwife were unable to say whether Lisa had a son or a daughter. The baby's genitalia had not developed correctly. Technically, this newborn had ambiguous genitalia, meaning it would require genetic testing to determine the baby's sex.

I drove straight to the hospital after my midwife partner called me at home with this news. She described the situation. "It was so awful in the delivery room. No one could completely answer Lisa's questions. It was very, very hard for all the staff, but especially, of course, for Lisa. She's asking to see you, Dana. I knew you'd want to know about this. They've called in a specialist from Children's."

As an experienced midwife, the most challenging cases for me were the ones in which babies had birth defects. This realization filled my mind while I parked the car and took the elevator up to the maternity unit. As the doors opened, I recalled Lisa saying repeatedly throughout her pregnancy, "God, I hope I don't have a baby with a birth defect." It made me wonder, "Did she really know? And if so, how? Or was this just a coincidence?"

Walking towards her room, I anticipated that Lisa would be alone, just as she had been throughout all of her pregnancy. The baby's father broke off their relationship with news of the conception. Lisa, a well-educated woman, made the decision to become a single mom. Her family, although supportive, lived out-of-state, so she would be dealing with this heartbreaking set of complications all on her own.

156

I knocked on her door and opened it slowly. Lisa looked up and cried, "Oh, Dana, you came."

"Of course. I came as soon as I got the call." My arms opened to give Lisa a big hug. Tears filled our eyes as we held our embrace. I kept her hands tightly in mine and sat next to her. "Lisa, I'm so sorry this has happened. We'll get through this together. What can I do for you right now?"

"Dana, I love this baby. All I know is there are a lot of problems and no one can tell me what's going on. As much as I want my baby to live, I don't want it to suffer through all sorts of crazy medical procedures." She paused and then reacted to her own words. "Oh my goodness, Dana, did you just hear me? I called my baby an 'it.' I can't even say him or her!" She sobbed in my arms.

"Lisa, this is one of the most difficult situations a new mom can face. How about if I go to the nursery and see what I can find out for you, okay?" I asked.

"That would be so wonderful, Dana. The not knowing is excruciating." Her voice trailed off. "Thank you so much for being here."

Dr. Lake, a specialist from Children's Hospital, arrived promptly to evaluate Lisa's baby. I introduced myself as we both washed our hands and put on cover gowns before entering the nursery. He confided to me, "Often these kids have kidney problems and a myriad of other structural defects." He did a comprehensive exam of the baby and ordered some tests which verified his initial concern. Lisa's baby had been born with multiple physical deformities.

I explained the situation to him, "This is a mother who all along has had a terrible fear that something bad was going to happen to her baby. Right now she's asking me, 'Should I do something to save this baby?' She doesn't want the baby to go through a multitude of medical interventions if it's not going to live."

He paused, "Well, I don't know. What can I say? Honestly, I really don't know."

I pushed the subject and asked more personally, "If you were the parent in this case, what would you do?"

He answered without any hesitation, "I would do nothing."

157

I replied, "That's exactly what I need to know."

Returning to Lisa's room, I shared Dr. Lake's findings with her. The baby had a meningocele, a part of the spine that did not close completely. The baby also had other major physical abnormalities. Soon Dr. Lake joined us and discussed the situation in more detail. He described all the treatment possibilities, itemizing the pros and cons of each. He didn't sugar coat any of it and told Lisa precisely what she was facing. Dr. Lake answered every question completely and honestly so that she could make an informed decision. When Lisa seemed to run out of questions, we gave her some time alone to consider all the options.

I grabbed a cup of coffee in the cafeteria and returned to Lisa's room. I sat at her bedside and simply listened as she talked through each option. Then she paused and quietly stared out the window in deep contemplation.

After a while, Lisa turned back to me. "I don't understand it, but deep down inside, I *knew* this was going to happen. From day one, I sensed that something about this pregnancy was not right. Call it intuition. Whatever it is, it doesn't feel at all like a mere coincidence to me."

Five days later, we sent Lisa home with her baby. It was very clear to her, to the physicians, and to our midwife practice that she was taking this baby home to die. Lisa's mother flew in to be with her under these unusual and devastating circumstances.

Despite the poor prognosis, Lisa decided to breastfeed her baby. We called daily to see how they were doing. Breastfeeding was going well, and Lisa continued to report that her baby seemed stable. No major changes were apparent. No complications were arising yet.

About a week later, Lisa called our midwife office and reported, "The meningocele is healing."

"What?" I thought to myself, "It is not healing. It can't be. She doesn't know what she's seeing."

I told Lisa, "Bring your baby in. Let's see what's going on."

Lisa and her mother brought the baby in for us to see, and she was right. Miraculously the meningocele was healing!

158

We immediately called Dr. Lake, who asked them to come to his office right away. After evaluating this amazing development, he explained to Lisa, "With the meningocele healing, the spinal fluid is going to build up, which could lead to brain damage if nothing is done. I recommend that we place a shunt to solve this problem." He further explained, "Lisa, in my opinion, this is one intervention worth doing for now. And who knows? Maybe this baby has more miracles in store for us." Lisa agreed to the surgery, and Dr. Lake placed the shunt to prevent any fluid build-up around the brain.

Lisa's baby lived. In fact, not only did her baby live, but over time, the baby's mental status was found to be just fine. In fact, this child was absolutely brilliant–bright as a button. From genetic testing, Dr. Lake discovered that the baby was a girl. Lisa named her Celia, meaning heavenly.

During the next couple years Celia underwent numerous surgeries from the waist down. Dr. Lake carried her around on his shoulders at Children's Hospital for all to see. He announced to everyone, "Can you believe this amazing child? Isn't she wonderful?"

Lisa frequently brought Celia back to our office for visits. As a toddler, she crawled from room to room in our clinic, dragging her bottom behind her. While Lisa and I talked in my office, the nurse played with Celia and could hardly keep up with her.

"Celia truly is a miracle child!" I exclaimed.

"She certainly is," Lisa agreed, and then added, "You know, I'm still awed by my strong feelings during Celia's pregnancy. All along I knew things weren't right. What do you make of that, Dana?"

"You never really know," I responded. "As a midwife, I've seen it go both ways. I've had patients who say, 'I'm sure nothing will go wrong,' and just the opposite happens. I've also seen women just like you, who have a strong intuition about something which turns out to be exactly right, and it's absolutely astounding. For that reason, I always consider that a woman's instincts might be right."

"And," I continued, "As a midwife, I sometimes have an intuition or two also. Sometimes it's right on and sometimes it's not. I call it coincidental intuition."

We both chuckled, pondering powers we couldn't quite name or fully understand but which touched our lives in amazing ways.

I went on, "One thing I do know for sure is that women have a great power, and that power is called wisdom. When women realize they have this gift and start using it, they take off and move in new directions. Just like you. And just like Celia, our miracle baby."

Just then there was a knock on the door. "Are you done yet?" asked my nurse. She was holding Celia who promptly squirmed out of her arms and scooted down the hall. My coincidental intuition told me to just sit back and watch. Celia would show us just how far she could go, having already exceeded all of our expectations.

Conception Births a Friendship

Carolyn is a midwife and mother-to-be. Despite the business of her bustling Florida practice, Carolyn finds a way to make close connections with her patients.

We had the same due date, Jessica and I. Although I was her midwife, we became friends as well. We just clicked. Jessica saw me for every prenatal visit. However, because she had her share of medical complications, the obstetricians were also involved in her care.

When Jessica returned to my office, I teased her, "You have had *thee* worst pregnancy I've ever seen!" She had experienced hyperemesis–a severe form of nausea and vomiting in early pregnancy. When Jessica was finally feeling better at four months, she ate some seafood and got food poisoning. More vomiting ensued. This was followed by several episodes of premature labor. Later in the pregnancy, she was diagnosed with gestational diabetes which she controlled well with her diet.

During a later prenatal visit, while I was measuring her very pregnant belly, Jessica asked me, "Could you please be the midwife on call to deliver my baby, Carolyn?"

"Jessica, you know I'd love to be there. And you also know I'll be on maternity leave at that time," I reminded her. "But let's see how it goes."

Amazingly it worked out. The midwife on-call phoned me early in the morning to report that Jessica was in early labor. Although due for labor myself, I decided to go to the hospital. Jessica beamed with a huge smile when I entered the room. It seemed meant to be.

Jessica progressed well throughout the day and was ready to push by early evening. We estimated the baby's weight to be over seven pounds. As she pushed the baby's head delivered, immediately displaying the dreaded turtle sign, large puffy cheeks emerging very slowly over the perineum. My midwife training told me to be alert for shoulder dystocia. Just as I suspected, during delivery the shoulders got stuck. I instructed the nurse to call for the physician, who

161

immediately entered the labor room. Between the two of us, Jonathan was born. He was absolutely fine, weighing eight pounds twelve ounces. He was a big boy.

Although my heart was still racing, Jessica remarked, "Boy, you sure know how to stay calm, Carolyn. That was scary, wasn't it?"

"It sure was a surprise, but all is well," I reassured her, and then added with a smile, "And my only question is this: Where exactly did you hide that good-sized baby?"

The next day, I returned to the hospital to visit Jessica. A nurse came up to me and said, "Oh, Carolyn, it's so good you're here. Did you get the news about Jonathan?" She explained that he was having seizures. My first reaction was to question whether or not it was related to the delivery, just as all practitioners do when something goes wrong. I bombarded myself with questions. "Did I miss something? What could I have done differently?"

Seeing the neurologist in the nursery, I asked Dr. Parks about the diagnosis. He reassured me that Jonathan's seizures were due to a medical condition totally unrelated to the labor or birth.

I went in to see Jessica and gave her a big hug. She was in tears. "Carolyn, I don't know how Jonathan's going to be. It was so frightening when he had the seizure. His eyes rolled up into his head and he shook so. Dr. Parks will be seeing him every day, so that makes me feel better." We agreed to keep in close touch for progress reports. Soon Jonathan was stabilized on medication, and Carolyn took him home.

Two weeks later, I gave birth to my son, Galen. My husband and I brought him home from the hospital the next day.

While breastfeeding that afternoon, Galen began to shake and his eyes rolled upwards. His arms spread out stiffly. He was having a seizure.

My husband, an emergency room nurse, was with me. Both of us watched in shock, hardly able to take in what we were witnessing. We couldn't believe this was happening to our precious son and immediately brought Galen back to the hospital for an evaluation. Dr. Parks, the same neurologist who saw Jonathan, evaluated Galen.

162

And then it was Jessica's turn to visit me. She entered the waiting room, opened her arms, and held me. All I could do was sob. I knew that Jessica needed no explanation. She had been through this. She knew exactly what I was feeling.

It amazed me how Jessica was brought into my life. Little did we know we would both experience the same conditions with our newborn sons. We were there to comfort and support each other, and we got through it together.

And so had Jonathan and Galen. They were both doing just fine. Maybe they would become friends as well, just like Jessica and me. We had formed a bond that went far beyond a shared due date and into a lifelong friendship.

Forgiving Myself

Tina works with one other nurse-midwife in a small New Mexico town where she is confronted with an unresolved conflict from decades ago.

"Tina, I would like to talk with you," requested the woman on the other end of my phone. "Actually, I *need* to talk with you," she said firmly.

I didn't recognize her voice and interrogated myself quickly. "Who was this?"

Then she added, "I'm Mona Sanchez. I don't know if you remember me or not. You delivered my little girl twenty years ago. I want to talk with you about my birth experience."

A lump rapidly formed in my throat. Forget her? Of course not! I had never forgotten Mona's horrendous birth experience, especially my part in it. Memories washed over me–memories I had fiercely attempted to push down every time they crowded my consciousness for the past two decades. I used to relive the scene daily. It haunted me for years. I blamed myself for everything that happened on my shift that day. It still made me sad. I sat silent.

"Are you still there?" Mona asked.

"Yes. Of course I remember you, Mona." Stalling, I asked, "Would you like to talk sometime in the next couple of weeks?"

"I'd like to get together as soon as possible," she answered promptly, "I'm available any day this week."

It was tempting to say, "How about never?" But instead, I responded with weak enthusiasm, "Oh, okay, how about tomorrow at 4:30? Clinic should be over for the day. Can you come to my office?"

"I'll be there," Mona assured me.

"Great," came out of my mouth, but my stomach felt like it had been hit by a fast pitch baseball.

At the click of the phone, I lowered my head into my hands, elbows planted on the desk. As I closed my eyes, I sighed and sank back into my chair, replaying Mona's birth scene like it was yesterday.

Mona had an easy pregnancy. She was a good candidate for our birth center located across the street from the hospital. As a brand new midwife, I always became elated following a wonderful birth experience. Mona's delivery of her daughter was no exception. That was, until the placenta didn't deliver. We were admiring her baby's gorgeous curly black hair. While I held the clamp on the umbilical cord, attached to the placenta still inside, we talked about how smooth the labor and birth had been.

After fifteen minutes, I checked to see if the placenta showed any signs of separation from the inner wall of the uterus. There was no trickle of blood, no lengthening of the cord, no classic signs of separation at all. The uterus felt fairly firm. "Just wait." I remembered my midwife instructor's admonition, "Pulling too hard on the cord can cause the uterus to turn inside out. If that ever happens, you have a true emergency on your hands." Exercising patience, I once again turned my attention to the baby.

Thirty minutes is the standard time it takes for the placenta to detach. At the half-hour mark, I put a small amount of traction on the cord. I didn't think it was too much. "Ooooh," cried Mona, "I feel cramping."

"This could be your placenta delivering," I told her. "Give me a push to help the placenta come out," I instructed Mona. She screamed as I steadied the cord. The color suddenly drained from Mona's face. She fainted right there in the bed. Beads of perspiration began to collect on her forehead.

My nurse yelled, "Her pulse is rapid and her blood pressure is dropping." I stopped pulling to evaluate what was happening. There was minimal blood loss, but a mass of meaty muscular tissue as large as an inflated balloon was at the opening of her vagina. I paled immediately, realizing that the uterus had become inverted. My instructor's warning was playing out before my very eyes. The nightmare had started.

"Call Dr. Rodriguez–STAT!" I ordered.

165

Placing my hand into the vagina, I tried to push the uterus back into its correct position. Within a few seconds the nurse ran back into the room, "Dr. Rodriquez wants us to bring her to the emergency room right away. He will meet us there." The nurse and I moved Mona to a stretcher and raced across the street to the ER. "Thank goodness the hospital is so close by," I whispered.

The staff had a room waiting for us. Placing his gloved hand and arm into the birth canal, Dr. Rodriguez attempted to peel the placenta off the uterine wall. He worked hard to put the uterus back into its correct position, but it didn't stay. The uterus again prolapsed like an inverted balloon.

The hospital staff rushed Mona to the operating room. There the doctors tried a number of procedures to return the uterus to its right position, but nothing worked. Mona ended up with a hysterectomy. Following the surgery, she continued her care with the obstetrician. I never saw Mona again.

Back in the office, a tear trickled down my cheek. The dike then opened wide and sadness overwhelmed me. Questions flooded my mind. I realized that I didn't want to talk about it–ever. The pain and guilt were still raw even after all these years. This incident shouldn't have happened, but it did. And now I was being forced to talk about it, to face it with the woman who had been directly affected by my actions. And it was she who needed to talk. I could hear the urgency in her voice. "Why now?" I wondered.

That night, I talked at length with my husband about this case from long ago. We called an attorney friend and discussed my risk of being sued after all this time. Sleep was illusive. I lay awake trying to concoct a different ending. The new ending never came.

The following clinic day was uneventful. At about 4:30, the receptionist informed me, "Someone by the name of Mona is here to see you." Mona smiled softly, extending her hand as I greeted her in the waiting area. I escorted Mona to my office, offered her a chair, and closed the door.

"Thank you for seeing me," Mona began. "My psychiatrist encouraged me to pay a visit to you and talk about what happened twenty years ago. It still haunts me. I never got over the fact that I lost my uterus and couldn't have any more babies. It made me despondent." She continued, "My family and I moved to a new city, thinking it would be good to have a new start, a new outlook. Nothing seemed to help. The devastating loss of my fertility became a wall between my husband and me. I couldn't let go of my grief. It ruined my marriage. My husband finally divorced me."

Mona began to sob and shake. I rolled my chair next to hers and embraced her. She willingly accepted and held my hug. My own tears began to fall as I continued to listen. "I felt so guilty about losing my uterus. I kept replaying the scene, trying to make a different ending. I had so many unanswered questions. What would have happened if I hadn't pushed? What did I do wrong? Why did you pull so hard? I blamed you for all my troubles."

Mona released my embrace as she dried her eyes. She continued, "The bright spot was Sonia. She was a wonderful and healthy child. I am so proud of her. Sonia has grown into a bright, energetic, young professional woman who has just had a daughter herself. I think the birth of my granddaughter resurrected all my past feelings. I needed to face you and tell my story."

"I'm glad you did, Mona. I've been avoiding this for twenty years." My voice wavered. "I've pushed the guilt and pain down every time it surfaced. I actually needed to face this myself and face you. I was a young midwife at the time and since then have done hundreds of deliveries. Yours was the most traumatic experience of my career. I've never forgotten that you lost your uterus while under my care. I've also asked myself some of the same questions and blamed myself for all that happened. I've searched for a different ending."

"Tell me from your perspective what happened," Mona requested, as she rested back in her chair. I shared with her my memory and perception of the delivery incident, including every detail, every nuance, and the questions that circled my mind over the years.

Mona sighed deeply, "Well, for some reason, I sense that I'm better after talking to you about it. It feels like healing has started, after listening to you, to your perspective. I know it's been painful for you to share your truth with me. I greatly appreciate your honesty." She paused, and looked deeply into my eyes. "I feel freer than I've felt in years." Mona stood, holding me at arm's length, and added, "And I don't want either of us to feel bad about this anymore."

Hugging me, Mona said, "Let's make a promise to each other. Let's release the pain that has haunted us both for all this time. Let's forgive ourselves." She kissed my cheek and said goodbye. Just like that. Mona squared her shoulders, lifted her head high, and walked out of my office. I watched in amazement.

Sitting down in my chair, I took in all that had happened and told myself, "Tina, you have to follow Mona's example and forgive yourself." I walked into an exam room, looked at myself in the mirror, and stated, "Mona's forgiven you. I forgive you." I said good-bye to this harrowing memory. My guilt and pain were released.

Gathering up my briefcase, I followed Mona's lead and squared my shoulders, lifted my head high, and walked out of the office, feeling freer than I'd felt in twenty years.

Listen to Me

Nancy gives culturally sensitive care to women in a large metropolitan area. She provides a listening ear to the many women she serves.

"You listen to me. I come see you again?" Lia's request replayed in my head. It didn't seem that I said anything unique, but something must have sparked her comment. I thought back over our conversation.

Lia was my last appointment on that busy clinic day. She merely picked my name out of the yellow pages of the phone book to schedule her annual exam. I was running a few minutes behind, but that didn't seem to bother her. Introducing myself, I explained that we would begin with her medical history. Lia sat erect in the chair, her feet not able to reach the floor.

I began, "Let's get started. What brings you in today? Do you have any concerns?"

Her crisp accent revealed her Vietnamese heritage. "I want be sure I'm okay. I need pap and any other tests that you think I need. I was told last year I'm starting pre-menopause. The doctor put me on hormones, but I still have periods. I don't understand."

"All right. Let's see. What medications are you taking right now?"

Lia reported that she was taking a birth control pill and a vitamin. She added that sometimes she forgets to take the pills.

"How frequently do you miss pills?"

"Oh, mostly on weekends. I take my pills to work. Sometimes I forget to bring home with me."

"Okay, tell me more about yourself. How long have you been in the United States?"

"I come on boat from Viet Nam in 1978. I pregnant then. My first son come with me. My husband send me. He think it better for me to come to U.S. I know nothing. American family take us in. They take good care of us. They help

169

me find job. I very stressed without husband. I have baby boy early. He very sick, but okay now."

"Any other babies, Lia?"

Hanging her head she responded, "No, no others. Just two sons. My husband very sad. He want many children. But I tell him we have many grandchildren some day. He will be very proud."

"What type of work do you do?"

"I work at accounting firm. I very good with figures. My husband work very hard too. My sons in school. They get education. They make us happy."

I nod. "Do you have any allergies to medicines?"

"No."

"Do you have any past health problems, like heart, kidney, liver or lung diseases?"

"No. I very good health."

"How about surgeries?"

"No."

"Is there anything else you would like to talk about?"

"I sometimes sad. Lonely. I cry a lot. I wish mother, father here, but they killed in our country. My husband help. He understand."

"Does your sadness make it difficult to complete your daily activities?"

"I no understand."

"Because you are sad, does that make you not get up and go to work? Does it stop you from eating or going to the store or cleaning your house?"

"Oh, no, Miss Nancy. I do all those things."

"Okay. That's what I wanted to know. Do you want to see a doctor about your sadness?

"No, I okay." We talked further about resources that might help.

"Let's do your exam. I'll step out for a minute. Here is a gown for you to put on. You can hang your clothes on those hooks and then sit up here on the table."

During the exam, I found her uterus to be enlarged, the size of a basketball.

When I told Lia, she remarked, "Yeah, I noticed open more. I thought it normal."

"I don't understand, Lia. What do you think is open more?" I pulled out my charts with pictures of the female anatomy. "Can you show on this diagram what you think is open?" Lia pointed to the vaginal opening.

"Oh, I understand now. Yes, sometimes the opening to the vagina gets a little larger with each baby. That is normal, but let me show you what I found on your exam." Pointing to the uterus, I added, "This is what has grown larger." Lia's eyes widened when I used my hands to demonstrate how large her uterus was.

"I am going to order some tests–some blood work and an ultrasound."

"What is ultrasound?"

I tried to describe the procedure that would be done in the office the next day. "It takes a picture of what is inside you. Then, you will see the doctor early next week. He is a gynecologist. He'll take good care of you. Here is your appointment."

"No. I come see you. You listen to me."

"Lia, it's important that you keep the visit with Dr. Apollo. He is a specialist and knows how to take care of you." The frown on her face made me continue. "I think there is something wrong. We need to do more tests. I trust him. He will take good care of you. I will tell him all about you. Promise me that you will keep the appointment."

"But I still see you?"

"You can come to see me again if any new concerns come up. But you must see Dr. Apollo on Tuesday at one o'clock for this problem. Do you understand?"

Lia hung her head and then nodded a yes. "Will the doctor listen to me?"

Knowingly, I responded, "Yes, Lia. I will talk to him before your appointment. He will listen to you, just like I listen."

171

The next week, Dr. Apollo notified me of his findings and the need for a hysterectomy. Lia's surgery was already scheduled for the following week. With a twinkle in his eye he said, "By the way, I told Lia that she could see you for the post-op visit on a day that we are both in clinic." My eyebrows rose as he smiled and shared, "I understand that you listen to her."

Chapter 6: Life With Death

Death may imply an ending, but along with the pain of loss, a new beginning always evolves. It is inevitable. These stories address the impact of death–from sudden to impending, from recent to long ago. And most appropriately, this chapter and this book so aptly conclude with a touching story titled *Hug*.

Over My Dead Body

Encouraged by her husband to obtain a college degree, Robin begins her educational journey. Then life deals her an unexpected blow.

"If we hadn't admitted Robin into the nursing program, what would she have done?" That's what the Dean of Nursing asked my neighbor as they stood together in the church balcony. Following the funeral, the dean watched me walk down the aisle with my six small children. My husband Donny died unexpectedly on Christmas Day. He was thirty-nine.

A few years before Donny's death, a night nurse had encouraged me to go back to school. I was working with her as a nurse's aide at our local hospital.

"I can't," I replied, "I've got six kids."

She promptly responded, "Robin, I don't care if you have a dozen. Do something. Don't stay in this job when you have the ability to do so much more. I've watched you. You have a lot of potential. Don't get stuck here."

So I decided to become a Licensed Practical Nurse. When my husband, Donny, heard my plans, he asserted, "Over my dead body. If we're sending you back to school, you're going to college and you're going to get a degree." So, when my youngest was nine months old, I enrolled in college and began taking the required general classes.

A couple years later, I applied to nursing school. However, the admissions board refused my application. I didn't know what to do. Had it not been for my chemistry professor, I would've dropped out right then and there.

"Why are you leaving the university?" he inquired.

"The admissions board told me that I shouldn't be a nurse because I'm married, I'm the mother of six kids, and at thirty-four, I'm 'too old.' They're concerned that I cannot carry on my *wifely duties*," I answered with a hint of sarcasm in my voice.

His eyebrows rose as he declared, "Well, we simply won't tolerate that kind of nonsense! Robin, I urge you to reconsider and try again. Please send in

174

your application one more time."

The next semester, I followed my chemistry professor's recommendation and reapplied to the nursing program. Coincidentally, he happened to sit on the Board of Admissions at the time. He later explained that when my application came up, he looked at it, and then peered around the room at each of the board members. They sat quietly around the table and for some unapparent reason, didn't comment. He then stated matter-of-factly, "Well then, I guess we'll try her."

It was in the middle of my nursing studies that Donny died of a sudden heart attack. A year later, I completed my undergraduate degree and started working evening shifts back at the local hospital. During the daytime hours I continued to run Donny's business, a meat locker plant. And, most importantly, I was raising six kids by myself. Sleep was practically nonexistent.

One day a friend called. She asked if I would like to commute with her to get a master's degree in nursing at a university two hours away.

"Over my dead body," was my first reaction, but I stopped myself. I would forever hear those words in Donny's voice, encouraging me to get a degree. Instead, I replied with tired cynicism, "Great. Between two and four in the morning I'll be there."

She challenged, "Well, I don't think you should be cutting meat all of your life."

Her comment forced me to reevaluate all that I was doing. I decided to cut back on my evening hours and take her up on the offer. For the next few years we drove two hours each way and completed our master's degrees in nursing administration. Afterwards, I sold the locker plant and found a job as a Director of Nursing, my job for the next ten years. I wondered what Donny would think of all this.

It amazed me how many brochures came across my desk for no apparent reason. One was from a nurse-midwifery program in the south. The idea of a master's degree in midwifery intrigued me. I looked at it over and over again. "Maybe I should go," I pondered. By this time my youngest was just finishing high school. Finally I decided to call the program and check it out. They said that one of their applicants had just dropped out of the program. Without even taking a second to think more about it, I took the spot.

Before leaving for Atlanta, I visited Donny's grave. "I will always remember your words, Donny," I said to him. "I've gone on to get my master's in nursing and now, I'm going get another one and become a nurse-midwife. You'd be proud of me, Donny. You're the one who believed in me and gave me the push I needed. Without you, what would I have done?"

Mirror Pregnancies

Julia, a nurse-midwife and mother of two children, provides prenatal care in a busy suburban practice where many of her patients return for subsequent pregnancies.

"Take a breath in, Sharon. Good. Now let it out slowly. Wonderful." Then I added, "Everything is okay." Sharon needed to hear that. All mothers longed to hear that. As a midwife, I had spoken these words to hundreds of women in labor. But on this particular morning, Sharon *really* needed to hear that everything was okay this time.

She lay on her side in the dimly lit birthing room, covered by a white sheet. Her eyes were closed and her brow furrowed. Sharon dozed between contractions which had become intense over the past couple hours. Sharon's husband, Charles, sat on a stool with one hand in hers and the other tenderly encircling her head. Their best friend Claudia wet the washcloth and placed it on Sharon's flushed and rosy cheeks.

My foot tapped lightly to the beat of the fetal heart which was keeping a perfect rhythm from the bedside monitor. Earlier that morning I had similarly tapped the brakes of my car while approaching the icy bridge on my way to the hospital. Christmas lights were strung between the lamp posts guiding me over the Mississippi river. This was where I mentally moved from my personal life to my calling as a midwife, anticipating the twelve hour shift ahead.

During this morning's mental transition, I took an extra pause. Not quite one year ago, I drove over this same bridge expecting a normal labor and delivery for Sharon. But it didn't happen the way we expected. That baby, Sharon and Charles's daughter, had stopped moving one month before her Christmas due date. She was born without a heartbeat at Thanksgiving. They named her Grace.

This year I sat on the edge of the bed in my blue scrubs and placed a hot pack on Sharon's back. The conversation was subdued now, unlike the excited chatter when Sharon first arrived.

177

When given the freedom to choose, a laboring woman will find the position that best helps with the delivery of her baby. Earlier that morning, Sharon had moved from the solid, wood rocking chair to the shower. Warm water flowed over her pregnant belly like a waterfall, soothing her labor pain. Now nestled in bed with pillows all around her, she found her spot.

"Take in some air. Now let it out slow." Sharon's hypnotic breathing suddenly came to a halt. I looked up. A catch in her breath was followed by a low, earthy grunt. I was surprised by this sign of progress so soon. The pushing stage was what we had been waiting for. This began my favorite part of labor–the anticipation of nine months peaking with the birth of a new life. Sharon and Charles, however, knew what it was like when that anticipation ended in tragedy. I searched Sharon's face, wondering what she was remembering from her previous stillbirth delivery of Grace. She took a long smooth breath and closed her eyes.

I thought back to the beginning of this pregnancy when Sharon sat in my office and asked with a quiet urgency, "Julia, can I see you every week?" The timing of this baby was like a reflection in the mirror, a glaring reminder of the year before. With this baby having the same due date as Grace, Sharon had been caught off guard. It added a whole new dimension to this pregnancy and to the pain of her previous loss.

"Of course you can," I responded without hesitation. My morning drives to this Friday clinic had me wondering each week how Sharon would be. I pondered what she would need to talk about and contemplated what words could possibly help heal the wound in her soul, still open and raw.

During these prenatal visits, we shared tears–not always midwife to patient, but also mother to mother. Sharon shared her deepest lows, the thoughts that she might be going crazy with grief and emotions. While she tried to cope with the recent loss of her baby, a new life continued to grow inside her.

Sharon talked a lot about Grace. It was clear from her conversations that this daughter would always be a part of their family history, never to be forgotten. Sharon lent me the videotape of Grace's memorial service. Family and friends had filled the pews. Charles spoke eloquently about the daughter who had entered their lives so briefly and whose spirit would live on forever.

During her prenatal visit on the Friday before Thanksgiving, I listened intently as Sharon anticipated this first anniversary of Grace's entrance into the world, just a couple days away. She sat across from me at the exact point in gestation as the year before. We listened to the strong fetal heart rate for an extra few minutes that day.

For this year's Thanksgiving holiday, Sharon and Charles declined the traditional family dinner and chose instead to have tacos and tortillas with friends. Breaking from tradition seemed fitting for what had broken in their hearts, and this was a step toward mending.

Following this tough anniversary, I began to hear a new voice emerging from Sharon. She spoke with new courage and hope. The tension that built up over the last few months was replaced with a determination to move on, a consideration of new possibilities, and an acceptance of new life.

My hand lightly touched the top of Sharon's abdomen where I could feel the strength of her contractions. The next one confirmed what I already knew from her voice. The initial wave began. She caught her breath. The involuntary reflex caused the uterine muscles to bear down under my fingertips. It was a force of nature that could not be stopped or controlled.

Sharon looked at me with her eyes wide open and eyebrows raised high. She had been here before. She knew it was time to push. I stared into her eyes. We connected. "The pushing urge will get stronger. Your body is doing exactly what it should be doing. Trust and listen to your body. You can do this, Sharon."

I gently checked her cervix and found that it was completely dilated. Clear water continued to leak out, another sign that this baby was doing just fine. "Sharon, you're moving fast. Let's get ready to have a baby." Once more I reassured her, "Everything is okay." She nodded, knowing exactly what those words meant.

A spark of energy ignited the room. Sharon moved to her back with her head raised. She placed her hands on her knees, getting ready for the next

179

contraction. Charles helped to adjust the pillows, supporting her head and back. Claudia gave her a sip of water. I lowered the foot of the bed to prepare for the birth.

"Julia, it's starting," she said. She was strong and pushed well. I moved the delivery table close behind me. My instruments were ready. After slipping on a white cover gown and sterile gloves, I stood at the end of the bed, watching and waiting.

Sharon's eyes closed as she gathered her strength for the next contraction. She did not notice the nurse who turned on the warmer of the isolette and checked the oxygen and suction tubing. Just in case.

Breath sounds, accelerating contractions, the fetal heart rate: the rhythms of labor were all peaking as the baby maneuvered through the birth canal toward its first breath. The room melted away. The focus was solely on Sharon.

"Augh!" The next contraction built quickly.

"Go ahead and push," I said. "Now, take a breath and push again. Keep listening to your body. That's it. Now take a break and wait for the next one."

The next five minutes of contractions came hard and strong, piling up close together.

"You're doing it. Keep going," I encouraged.

The perineum began to bulge and I moved closer. The labia separated with each push to reveal a small dot of dark hair which magically enlarged before our eyes. "The head's beginning to crown."

Sharon's eyes were closed. There was no time to think now. Charles and Claudia huddled closely on each side of her, ever encouraging and supporting.

I placed one hand gently on the perineum, now stretched paper thin around the baby's head. My other hand pressed down slightly on the head from above to keep it flexed. "Time to stop pushing. Do some light puffs now." The perineum slipped easily under the baby's chin. The head was born and began to rotate, with the round pink cheeks following. The baby's eyes were open and blinked at me as if to say, "I'm okay." I smiled.

180

But Sharon was not okay. She looked at Claudia and then to me with eyes wide with panic. "The baby's not crying," Sharon stated with a whispered terror. She leaned forward, peering over her belly, straining to see the baby's head. "He looks blue!"

Her reaction caught me off guard for just a second. "Your baby's doing fine, Sharon. This is normal," I reassured her.

My clinical side took over my thoughts for the delivery. "Suction the mouth, then the nose. Check for the cord around the neck. Slip it over the head. Gently and steadily press down to deliver the first, anterior shoulder. Good. It's coming easily."

I paused. "Now, Charles, place your hands here by mine." He did, touching the wet hair of his baby.

With his hands on mine, I lifted upwards. The posterior shoulder delivered smoothly. Then, with one continuous motion, a beautiful newborn emerged from Sharon's body. I suctioned the baby's mouth and nose further, taking an extra moment to make sure he made a smooth transition to this new world. He did.

Charles and I lifted him into Sharon's waiting arms, which surrounded his body like a ribbon around a priceless gift. She pressed her son close to her heart. Ben was here. He was alive. Quiet tears filled the room. My own vision blurred with tears. Joy and relief overwhelmed us all with this new life.

It was dark when I left the hospital, feeling both exhausted and euphoric. My foot pressed on the gas pedal as the bridge carried me up and over the icy Mississippi. Christmas was only a few days away, but in my mind it had already arrived with the birth of Ben, a birth that would forever be etched in my mind and heart. I momentarily checked my rearview mirror to glance behind me, reflecting on Sharon's "mirror pregnancies." I let out a big sigh. Yes, everything was okay this time.

181

Cradled Again

Maureen lives in a rural river town approximately a hundred miles from the "Big City," where tragedy hits close to home.

I didn't pay much attention to the sirens that morning, but I immediately stiffened when my husband said, "There's been an accident."

Carl, a local policeman, would only call me with such news if I knew the person. Panicked, I pelted him with questions, "What did you say? Who was involved? What happened?"

"It's little Meg. She accidentally got hung on some twine in the barn. Jim found her dangling from the loft." His voice quivered, "Maureen, it's not good. They've airlifted her to the university hospital." Carl then shared the rest of the details.

"I have to get dressed and head to the hospital to be with Carol and Jim." I was too stunned to cry. Meg was very special to me.

Racing to the city, I remembered when Carol was pregnant with Meg four years ago. After the delivery, I cradled Meg in my arms before handing her to my best friend and neighbor. From day one she looked like an angel with a halo of light blonde curls and sparkly blue eyes. Her perky energy brought joy to all who met her. She always had a hug for everyone in our small community. We were one big extended family.

Arriving at the hospital, fear filled my heart. What would be happening? I asked for directions to the pediatric intensive care unit. The receptionist told me to take the main elevator to the third floor, make two right turns, then a left, and follow the signs. The hugeness of this place was overwhelming.

Carol and Jim spotted me as I approached the desk. They threw their arms around me and began to sob. Trying to keep my composure, I asked the nurse where the waiting room was located. With my arm around Carol, we entered the small area and sat down.

"The doctors keep doing tests, and they all tell us the same thing. Meg is brain dead," Jim informed me, choking up. He continued, "We've decided to donate her organs."

Nothing during my drive had prepared me for this.

"Maureen," Jim asked, "Will you go to the operating room with Meg when they harvest her organs? You were there when she was born, and we want you to be with her at the end. We don't want her to be alone, but we just can't do it."

Their request took my breath away. I hesitated and then responded as tears filled my eyes, "Of course. I'll do this for you both, and for Meg."

The nurse showed me where to change into scrubs. They looked just like the ones I wore for deliveries back home. Returning to the surgical holding area, I found Carol and Jim leaning over Meg's stretcher, giving her kisses between all the tubes, machines, and IV lines. Tenderly, they caressed her face and said a final good-bye. It all seemed to be happening so fast. Too fast.

Surgery personnel swiftly maneuvered the cart into the elevator. I followed along, taking several deep breaths, unable to fight back my tears. I held Meg's hand as we entered the operating room suite.

The team of doctor's introduced themselves and gave me a stool to sit on. They began the surgery. Still holding Meg's hand, I leaned down and whispered in her ear, "Meg, you are in good hands. I'll be here with you the whole time. In fact, I promise to write a letter to your Mom and Dad from the two of us so that they'll know about these last moments of your life. I'll try to make it your words Megan, as best I can."

Knowing I would compose this letter for Carol and Jim helped me to cope and stay focused on the procedures. I tried to frame the words so that my friends would understand the contribution their little girl was making, hoping that somehow this would bring them some comfort down the road. My pen touched the paper:

My Dearest Mommy and Daddy,

183

Thank you for everything you have done for me. You made my stay on earth just perfect. I can't wait for when we will all be together in heaven. I want to tell you about my last couple of hours. I was so eager to try on my angel wings, but had to wait for the transplant team. Thank you for sending Maureen to be with me.

When you kissed me good-bye at the elevator doors, I was not afraid. I will always love you.

When they wheeled me into the surgery room, the crew was ready. They moved swiftly and gently. Each person commented on my golden hair and how pretty it was. They also praised you, Mommy and Daddy, for being so strong and courageous. We are doing a brave thing, aren't we?

When surgery started, my blood pressure dropped. I must have been in a hurry to start playing in heaven. The doctor at the head of the table gave me some medicine. Maureen prayed and reminded me to hang onto my body for just a little while longer. With everyone's prayers, I was able to stay calm and wait until it was the right time. You know me. I've always got places to go and things to do!

The two transplant doctors asked about me. Maureen told them all the stories she had heard. Maureen also shared that she was the midwife when I was born. One of the doctors just had a baby boy about nineteen weeks ago. Well, actually, his wife had the baby by c-section. Maureen sure likes to talk about babies!

The transplant coordinator came in and told me that a teenage boy was going to get my pancreas and that he was not going to be diabetic any more. They also said that a lady was getting my liver and she was already on her way to a hospital in another state–all while I was in surgery. My eyes will help someone else be able to see and play games with his family just like we did.

The doctor said that my organs were perfectly shaped and the size was right even for adults to receive.

Maureen rubbed my head and kept my teddy bear near me the whole time. Finally, at 6:45, my heart was given to another little girl whose heart was hurt by a bad virus. When my heart stopped, I was finally released to go to heaven. Maureen kissed my head. She sent me love from all my family and friends at that very moment.

I have pretty green stitches on my chest and tummy. They tenderly wrapped my body in warm blankets. I was so surprised the nurses were crying. They gave me a hug and told me how brave I was. The doctor also got very quiet and gave my shoulder a little squeeze, saying they would take very good care of my organs. I saw a tear in his eye too. Then they called the pilot, and the carrier hurried his special cargo to the airport.

I am so happy for our four wonderful years together. My life was short, but I loved every minute of it. Don't be sad for too long. You have to take care of my little sissy, Nicole. She needs you both. Please tell her how much I love her when she gets a little older.

I'm not scared or sad. I'm not in any pain. I am resting in peace, knowing that you love me and that you will keep me in your hearts forever.

Remember, I will always be your little angel,

Love forever,

Meg

I asked the nurse to provide Carol and Jim with a private waiting room and a rocking chair. The operating room nurses covered Meg's body with an extra blanket. The surgeon gently placed her in my arms. Once again, I cradled Meg. Then I entered the waiting room and tenderly delivered Meg to her mother's waiting arms.

Celebration

Jeanne questions why she wasn't chosen to attend the second birth of one of her favorite clients.

"Jeanne, grab your coat. We're going to a party!" ordered Dr. Totino. His beaming smile contrasted with my furrowed brow and questioning look.

Hardly catching a breath, he quickly explained, "Carla's had another baby! She's at the birth center on Broadway and sent Juanita over to get us. Juanita's so excited for her sister and Jose. They've had a healthy little girl. Carla wants us to come and join the party. After all, we are family, aren't we? Let's get going!"

Hurrying to my office, I threw on my coat and headed for his car. As Dr. Totino sped down the highway to the birth center I sat silent, engrossed in my own thoughts. "Carla had another baby? I didn't even know she was pregnant. Why didn't Carla come back to us for her prenatal care? Why didn't Juanita tell me? I just saw her saw her at the supermarket last month. All the Alvarado girls come to us for their pregnancies–Juanita, Nina, Maria, Lolita, and Carla. They're like our sisters."

Deep down I understood why Carla didn't want to return to us for her second baby. As rejected as I felt, I couldn't blame her.

I remembered the details of her first pregnancy like it was yesterday. Nina brought Carla in for her initial prenatal visit in the middle of her second trimester. As if reading my mind, Carla had explained to me, "I didn't come sooner because Jose and I don't have much money and no insurance. Now I have a full-time job with health insurance and Jose has been working two jobs to save money for the baby. He really wants to provide for us."

At Carla's next visit a month later, she complained of double vision. Since her blood pressure was still within normal range, I sent her to the ophthalmologist. He called promptly and informed me that her optic discs were slightly swollen. We agreed this finding was abnormal. I consulted with one of the obstetricians in our practice. We decided on a watch-and-wait approach with more frequent prenatal visits. I set up an appointment for the following week to recheck Carla's blood pressure. We also put her on bed rest at home.

Three days later, Carla made an emergency appointment with Dr. Totino because she didn't feel well. She was swollen from her head to her toes. Her blood pressure was elevated. But then the real shock came: There was no fetal heartbeat. We admitted Carla to the hospital and induced labor.

While seeing clinic patients that day, I couldn't stop thinking about the induction taking place, wishing I could be there with Carla. Several hours later, Juanita appeared at my office door.

"We want you do the delivery. Dr. Totino has been monitoring Carla's blood pressure and the medication she's receiving," Juanita explained. "He sent me to get you."

Dr. Garcia, another obstetrician in our office, overheard the conversation. "Jeanne, I'll see the rest of your patients. You go where you are needed most. Go. Be with Carla."

Rushing to the hospital with Juanita, I changed into scrubs and entered the birthing room. Juanita, Nina, and their husbands were gathered around Carla and Jose. Carla's soft crying broke the silence. When she realized I was at her bedside, Carla reached for me, collapsing into my open arms. She cried, "I'm so glad you are here. Please don't leave me."

"Don't worry, Carla, I'm not going anywhere." I settled into the rhythm of the room and gently rubbed her back. Guitar music played softly while she breathed in and out slowly to control her pain. It was only four hours before Carla gasped that she had to bear down.

Checking her cervix to make sure it was fully dilated, I encouraged Carla to push with the next contraction, lifting the last bit of cervix over the baby's head. She pushed with all her might. As the baby's head emerged, Carla began to cry again. I gently wrapped their stillborn baby boy in a blanket and placed him in his mother's arms. Everyone wept. Each member of the family took turns holding him. Whispering his love and sadness, Jose cradled his silent son.

187

A priest blessed and anointed the baby. The nurses gave Carla a lock of his hair, the blanket that wrapped him, his ankle bracelets, and a copy of his footprints. Then they completed all the procedures required for a stillborn infant.

After the family members left, I expressed my sympathy to Carla and Jose and described preeclampsia, a disease that often occurs with first pregnancies. "We will want to see you more frequently during your next pregnancy."

Dr. Totino's car turned off the freeway. My mind continued to drift, "We didn't even know about this pregnancy." Tears stung my eyes.

After parking the car, Dr. Totino interrupted my thoughts, "We're here!" He rattled the keys at me. I smiled weakly and followed him into the center.

His booming voice interrupted the chatter in the birthing room. "Here we are! Now, where is this new baby?" We were greeted with hugs.

Carla reached her hand to me. I gave her a big hug. "Congratulations are in order," I offered. I sat down on the edge of the bed and politely formed the words. "How did things go for you?" but I wanted to say, "Why didn't you come to us?"

As if she heard my silent question, Carla looked into my eyes. "Jeanne, the labor was so much harder than last time, maybe because the baby was so much bigger. I even went four days past my due date."

She spoke softer and elaborated, "You know, I believed that losing my first baby was all my fault. It seemed the stress of work contributed to the complications. So with this new pregnancy, I was determined to have a live baby so quit my job. Without any income, I had to apply for medical assistance. The social worker assigned me to this clinic for prenatal care. There was no choice in the matter. The midwives here took good care of me, but I sure missed you." Carla squeezed my hand. "Well, enough of my jabbering. We invited you and Doctor Totino here to help us celebrate. You are family to us."

Smiling at her husband, she demanded, "Jose, let me have my daughter." Jose reluctantly handed Carla their new baby girl, whose ebony eyes peeked out from her bundled blanket. Stretching out her hands, Carla placed her newborn into my arms, "I want you to meet our daughter, Carlotta. And Carlotta, I want you to meet your Tia Jeanne, my midwife."

Cradling the baby, it all made sense. My heart melted. I declared, "Welcome to the family, Carlotta. You have been born into one of the best. And maybe someday, I'll deliver your babies. We'll keep this celebration going for generations to come."

Saving Lupita

Rosa is driven to a career in midwifery as a result of providing care to an indigent woman in a small town near the Mexican border.

"Angie, get me that application. I'm going to midwifery school." I stood at the door of her office on a hot humid summer day. Angie was a midwife and my good friend. As a nurse practitioner, I consulted with her concerning many of my female patients, despite the fact that her practice was over an hour away. Angie was insightful and direct. She had the most expressive face I had ever seen.

"Is that right?" She raised one curious eyebrow. "What made you change your mind?" She shuffled through the stacks of papers on her desk trying to locate the application, "I know it's here somewhere..."

She paused momentarily and looked directly at me, eyes narrowed. "You've resisted going back to school for the five years I've known you. You will be a wonderful midwife, but you," she shifted into a perfect impression of me, "don't have the money, the time, or the energy to go back to school."

In her own voice, she continued, "Something very significant must have happened to change your mind. Sit down and talk to me. Come on, Rosa, out with it." Angie motioned me to a chair as she then sat back in hers, looking as if she were prepared to sit there all day.

I looked down at my feet. My hands gripped the arms of the oak chair. I sighed. Tears filled my eyes as I choked out my response, "A woman died because of me. If I had become a midwife, Lupita would be alive today." I wept softly with my face in my hands.

Angie's eyes widened momentarily. She sat quietly for a moment, and then slid a box of tissues across the desk. "Tell me about Lupita."

I blew my nose and began the story. "Lupita came to our migrant health clinic last month for help. She had lost her medical aid and couldn't go back to the family practitioner she had been seeing. She suspected that someone had told the agency the father of her baby was back in town. Because he had a job, the social worker terminated her Medicaid insurance."

I wiped my nose and continued, "Lupita was carrying twins and was already in her eighth month. Her blood pressure was a bit high, and her feet were swollen. I told her this clinic didn't provide prenatal care and emphasized that she must return right away to the doctor she had been seeing. I pleaded with her. Lupita kept shaking her head no and said she couldn't go back. She had no insurance and couldn't pay for the care."

"I found out yesterday that she delivered that very same night with a traditional birth attendant at home. The babies are okay, but later she hemorrhaged. They called an ambulance, but it was too late."

I paused to catch my breath. "Angie, if I had been a midwife, I could have prevented her death! If I had done the training, I would have known that her symptoms were more than serious—they were life threatening! I could have convinced her to go somewhere for medical care. She should have gone to the emergency room at the county hospital. They would have taken care of her." Tears rolled down my cheeks. "I feel so powerless and never want to feel that impotent again. I want to be a midwife."

Angie responded as she handed me the application form, "First of all, you are not to blame for Lupita's death. You did all you could to get Lupita to the appropriate provider. Second, as a midwife, I feel powerless just about every day. There are just some things we can't control, no matter how well trained we are. We do our best to help patients make the right decisions for their lives, but ultimately it's their choice." She went on, "There's a very strong likelihood that if you were a midwife, you wouldn't have been at that clinic. You never would have met Lupita. You never would have had this tragic, life-changing experience."

Angie's beautiful eyes filled with compassion and wisdom, "You are going to be a fabulous midwife, and you are going to help many, many women. You are even going to save lives. But you are also going to feel powerless from time to time. Some things are beyond our control and understanding."

She handed me the paperwork, back to business. "Let me know if you

191

need any help filling this out and be sure to add my name as one of your references. I'd better go check on my patient. She's probably wondering where I went!"

I knew Angie was right and began to let go of the guilt I had been carrying. Placing my pen on the midwife application form, I filled out each line, in honor of Lupita.

Fragile Trust

Gail is in the same midwifery practice as Eleanor, a Scottish midwife who relocated to the United States. Together they experience a tough lesson about trust while caring for a unique immigrant population.

Eleanor looked worried as she approached the Labor and Delivery counter. "Gail, I have a patient to add to your list." It was my day to be on call at the hospital. Eleanor, one of the calmest and most experienced midwives in our practice, further warned, "This is not good news." I pulled out my list filled with patient names–women who had called with labor questions, women who had already delivered, and pregnant women with special concerns. I began to write as Eleanor explained.

"Her name is Mao. She is a thirty-eight year-old Hmong woman who is pregnant for the seventh time. Mao and her husband are new refugees from the camps in Thailand. She is due in a week and her amniotic fluid level is extremely low. I've ordered a number of ultrasounds over the past month. They continue to show that the water around the baby is decreasing significantly."

Eleanor shook her head and continued, "I've tried so hard to convince them to come in for an induction and get this baby delivered, but they've refused. The amount of fluid is so low it's practically nonexistent. I don't know if this baby will survive. Gail, I've never seen anything like this." For Eleanor, a midwife who had practiced all around the world, this was a strong statement. I took it even more seriously coming from her.

"The doctors, including Dr. Brooks, know all about Mao and her refusal to be induced. I need to go home now, but if she happens to call with contractions, do your best to convince her to get to Labor and Delivery. Then call me right away. I'll come in to take care of her."

I penned three stars by Mao's name to emphasize the seriousness of her case, then folded up the list and stuck it in the pocket of my blue scrubs. "I'll call you immediately if we hear from her," I reassured Eleanor.

193

It was five o'clock. "Three hours left to my shift," I calculated. "I hope to see Mao before I go home this evening, for her baby's sake."

Since no one was in labor, I walked down the long deserted hall to our call room. I turned on the TV news and read through a midwifery journal. While I was listening to the headline stories, my beeper suddenly buzzed. I called Labor and Delivery. "Did you page me?" I asked the nurse.

"Yes," she replied, "It's a Hmong daughter calling in and interpreting for her mother. The patient's name is Mao. Hang up and I'll put the call through to you." I hung up the phone, and it rang a second later.

"Hello?" I answered.

A sweet but worried voice responded, "Hi. My mother thinks she might be in labor. She sees Eleanor. She says it's time."

I gathered a bit more information. My three stars jumped out at me. I realized that this was the patient that Eleanor was worried about.

"Please have her come in right away," I instructed. "Do you have transportation?"

"Yes," her daughter answered, "My cousin will drive her. We will leave right now."

I paged Eleanor immediately, thinking she had probably just arrived home and will now have to turn around and come back to the hospital. But I knew she would be more than happy to return for this patient. Since starting the Southeast Asian clinic, Eleanor came in for many of her patients. She worked very hard to develop trust with them, a population that was not used to Western medicine and technology.

Eleanor returned my call within a minute and was on her way back to the hospital. I walked back to Labor and Delivery and waited for this patient who had us both so worried. "This is good. It's good she's getting in tonight, before anything bad happens to her baby," I affirmed to myself.

Eleanor arrived just as Mao and her family came through the entrance. "Let's get you into a room," she said gently to Mao. "I'll help you."

I waited at the desk and reminded Eleanor, "Let me know if you need anything. I'll hang out here." She nodded. We both understood the Hmong were very shy and private. They didn't want too many people in the room. I also understood why Mao wanted Eleanor, the midwife who followed her through this pregnancy, and not someone new to care for her.

The nurses and I chatted at the desk, hoping for good news of progress from Eleanor. She would take her time with Mao and not rush her. The door opened. Eleanor called out in an urgent whisper, "Get Dr. Brooks and the ultrasound machine please–and hurry!"

We knew instantly that Eleanor was unable to hear the baby's heart beat with the hand-held doppler. I quickly wheeled the ultrasound machine into the room while the nurse paged Dr. Brooks, who arrived within seconds. I stepped out of Mao's room to give her the privacy she desired. At the desk, we sat in quiet anticipation and waited. Tension filled the air as it always did on the Labor and Delivery unit when a fetal heart beat could not be detected.

Dr. Brooks came out first, shaking her head slowly from side to side. Sadly she shared, "No. There is no heartbeat." She respectfully left Eleanor to discuss this tragic news with the patient and her husband. We stayed at the desk, not saying a word. Mao's labor room door remained closed.

About thirty minutes later, Eleanor came out and consulted with Dr. Brooks. "They do not believe the ultrasound results," Eleanor explained. "They think the baby is still alive."

Eleanor added that Mao was in active labor and would deliver soon. "I'll call if I need anything," she assured us. Eleanor went back into the room and closed the door. The nurse followed to prepare for the delivery.

All remained quiet on the Labor and Delivery unit for the rest of my shift. The phone didn't even ring. Later Eleanor came out to the desk, still wearing her cover gown. It was a silent birth.

She sat down and described what happened. "Mao and her husband continued to believe their baby was alive no matter what I said, no matter what the ultrasound showed. But their baby boy was born dead. We wrapped him in

195

blankets. It wasn't until Mao's husband actually held him and saw with his own eyes what I had been trying to say." Eleanor paused and then further explained, "In that moment he realized his son was truly dead. Gail, do you know what he said to me then? He said, 'We didn't trust you. We didn't believe what you told us about the low fluid.'" She paused soberly, "Then he said, 'We trust you now.'"

We sorrowfully reflected on the circumstances of the evening. Never, ever, did Eleanor wish to earn their confidence in this way–for this couple or for any of the Hmong people who settled into this part of the world.

Eventually, however, trust developed. Word of mouth spread the news among the Hmong community about this caring midwife. In fact, over the next few years, I could hear it in the voices of these Southeast Asian women who called Labor and Delivery. "My labor has started," they would announce, and then add with pride, "I see Eleanor."

What If

Fran, an experienced midwife, lives in a costal Maine town. Daily she encounters women with unanswered and unanswerable questions.

"Fran, this baby sure moves a lot," Judy remarked as I entered the exam room.

As I sat down on the round exam stool and faced her, Judy fired one question after another. "What if the cord gets wrapped around this baby's neck? What if there's another cord accident like the last time? What if this baby dies? What if..." her questioning voice trailed off but boldly returned, "what if it happens again?"

"Judy, many women have these same fears during pregnancy," I gently pointed out while placing my hand on her forearm and giving it a squeeze. "But they're much worse for you because of your past experience. You've lived the reality of having a baby die in your womb. You know the devastation, the loss of all your dreams for your child."

Tears formed quickly and trickled down her cheeks. I waited patiently for her to continue. Judy sighed, "You're right. When I lost James, I lost a piece of my heart. It's terrifying to think it could happen again. It feels overwhelming nearly every waking hour."

"It's natural and normal for you to worry, Judy. Every mother worries a little. And telling you to stop worrying is easier said than done." I handed her a tissue, "What can I do to help?"

Judy blew her nose and responded, "Just the fact that you take the time to listen is helpful. Bill gets tired of me talking about this all the time. I know he worries too, but he doesn't like to talk about it."

"You know you can call me anytime, right?" I confirmed with her.

"Yes, I do know that. Thank you, Fran." She smiled weakly.

I changed the subject. "Let's have you lie back so we can check this baby out."

197

After measuring the height of the uterus and palpating the baby's position, I reached for Judy's hands and taught her how to find the baby's head, back, and legs. The baby kicked under her fingertips, and we saw a little bump protruding across her tummy. Amused, Judy emphasized, "See, I told you this baby moves a lot." Together we listened to the baby's heartbeat for over a minute.

I smiled and reassured her, "The baby's heart beat is 144. It's regular and strong."

Tears fell again from her eyes. I helped her sit up, handed her another tissue, and gave her a hug. "Remember, call me anytime. I mean it. And, it's time to start checking things more frequently. Let's schedule your next visit in two weeks. We'll stay on that schedule 'til 34 weeks. Between now and then, keep up the fetal movement counts. Don't hesitate to call if your baby is moving less frequently."

Nodding agreement, Judy answered, "I will. I promise." She added with a smile, "I feel better now that we've talked."

Judy and I spoke every week. She called often to report her baby's fetal activity along with her concern that there was either too much movement or not enough. I listened intently and gave reassurance, further explaining that as the baby grew there would be less room for him to move around. The activity would still be happening, but it could feel a bit different. I gently teased, "Judy, you won't be satisfied, will you, until this baby is in your arms?"

"You got it," she replied, and then added, "Speaking of a baby in my arms, I talk to this one every night."

"Really?" I prompted her, "What do you say?"

Judy's voice grew warmer, "Your daddy and I love you so much. I can tell from your kicks that you're growing stronger every day. Oh, I long to see you alive and healthy and can't wait to hold you in my arms."

"Oh Judy," I sighed, "That's beautiful. It's such a strong and fearless affirmation to your child and yourself."

"So, Fran, when do you think this baby will come? When am I going to hold my baby in my arms?" she questioned with anticipation.

198

"Well if I could predict that for everyone, I'd be a millionaire," I responded.

Judy chuckled, "I'll give you a million if you make this baby come soon."

"How I wish I could do that, but you know that labor will happen when it's ready. Trust your body. It knows the right time," I reminded her.

As Judy's due date approached, the phone calls increased. I heard an escalating tension in her voice. Even though her baby was still doing flip-flops and high karate kicks in her womb, she was having flash backs to her previous pregnancy when the baby's movements suddenly stopped without warning. Her current due date had arrived, and she was getting discouraged.

I repeated the same instructions. "The fetal stress test looked great. Trust your body. Have faith in yourself and your baby. It will happen."

Four days past her due date, I received a call from Judy. Her joyful voice said it all. "Fran, I'm in labor. It really is happening! Can you believe it?"

"Of course," I remarked, "I'll meet you at the hospital. Now get going."

"Bill and I are on our way," she informed me and laughed nervously, "The baby is still moving lots."

When I arrived at the hospital, the charge nurse directed me to the labor room. Judy and Bill were studying the heart rate tracing. "How's your baby doing?" I asked.

With a deep sigh Judy responded, "Just like you always say: 'Looks good.' What do you think?"

"Yes, it looks *really* good," I answered. "How about going for a walk?" For most of the labor, the three of us walked the halls, stopping to allow Judy to breathe rhythmically during the hard part of the contractions.

We stopped every few minutes and listened to the baby's heart rate. "Always nice and strong, this baby of yours," became the theme of the day.

Finally, the contractions dramatically escalated, and we settled Judy in bed. I performed one more check and found that the cervix was completely dilated. As I began to withdraw my gloved finger, amniotic fluid spilled out with a gush. "Whoops!" I yelped. "It's not going to be much longer now."

199

Judy started to laugh and then gasped, "I have to push!"

"That was a good one! The head is already crowning. Let's see if we can slow the next one down so you don't tear," I instructed.

As Judy questioned, "Are you sure the baby is okay? Is the cord...?"

I interrupted and reassured her, "Judy your baby looks great. It's time to focus on giving birth."

With the next contraction, she pushed lightly while I applied gentle pressure against the perineum.

A few more questions surfaced from Judy, "What if the cord is around the baby's neck? What if it gets pulled? What if the baby gets stuck? What if the baby won't come out?"

"Judy listen to me. All is well. Let's push this baby out," I encouraged. "Here comes a hard contraction. We're ready. Go for it!"

The head was born quickly and the little face puckered. I instructed, "Judy, your baby is already trying to cry. Give me your hands."

Together we lifted her squalling pink baby to her chest. Judy rested her head back on the pillow and began to weep with relief. Bill cut the cord and the nurse tucked a warm blanket over mother and child.

The baby suddenly kicked his feet so hard that the blanket unwrapped. "And you are right!" I announced, "This baby does move a lot!"

For the first time in nine months, Judy simply laughed.

Hug

Nina, a nurse-midwife for over twenty years in a busy Hispanic community, receives a special and unexpected gift during an otherwise uneventful clinic day.

A handsome young man suddenly filled the expanse of my office doorway. I looked up and couldn't help but notice his blue eyes and curly blond hair topping his tall muscular frame. "Are you Nina Fischer?" he inquired.

I took a step backward but didn't recognize him. Questions raced through my head. "Who was he? Why was he here? What does he want with me?"

Hesitantly I replied, "Why yes, I am. How may I help you?"

His white teeth sparkled from a wide grin as he answered my question. "I have a gift for you from my mom," he explained.

My curiosity was piqued, but more unspoken questions flashed through my mind, "Who's your mother? A gift? Your hands are empty!"

He continued excitedly as he stepped forward, "I am so happy to have finally found you! I am here to fulfill my mother's last request."

With that startling comment, he reached down to me. His strong arms wrapped around my petite frame. His upper arms pressed gently around my shoulders as his forearms crossed my back and stayed there for a few seconds. His hands softly squeezed the sides of my body like a child hugging a familiar stuffed animal. I thought, "The Velveteen Rabbit would understand this hug!"

A second shorter embrace followed the first. These warm hugs conveyed all the tender love and compassion of a son for his mother. "Thank you, from my mom," he whispered as he took a short step backward.

Unprepared for this demonstration of affection, I looked up curiously at this mysterious young man. Holding him at arms' length, I declared, "There is a story here and I would love to hear it. Please sit. Tell me who you are."

201

He sat down in the easy chair and began to explain. "I am Robert Rendquist. My mother was Angela Rendquist. You delivered me seventeen years ago." He hesitated as tears filled his eyes, and then clarified, "My mother died of cancer six months ago. Before she died, she told me, 'Find Nina. Give her a hug for me.' So I came and found you."

Robert continued as tears fell gently down his cheeks. "As I grew up my mom told me the story of my birth over and over again. She wanted me to know how special you had made my birth for her. My mom was only sixteen at the time, but you made a big impression on her. You cared for her at the free clinic in Harrington. She and my dad were very poor. You always made her feel welcome." Robert paused.

"Well, I try to do that with all my clients," I responded and then urged him, "Please continue."

"She said you always greeted her with a smile. You always took the time to answer her questions during the visits. I remembered she said you even put her in the big delivery room so that our whole family could be there for my birth. You recognized that family was important to her. And there were lots of relatives, seven in all: my dad, both my grandmas, and my mom's father and her sister. My dad's sister was there too. And my mom's favorite aunt from Louisiana came for the birth. It was such a celebration. My mom said there was joy and laughter when I was born. Every birthday, there was a party. She told me my birth was a big celebration, and she never let me forget it."

As he talked, I remembered the warm crowd of people filling the delivery room and the hearty family who welcomed this young man into the world.

Robert went on, "Soon after my birth, we moved up north where my dad was able to find a factory job." Choking up, he spoke softly, "Thank you for taking such good care of my mom. I'll never forget what you meant to her. I finally found the Nina that she always talked about and longed for me to meet."

I sat quietly, trying to comprehend all that he had shared with me. I was in awe of this young man who had traveled so far to find me. Tears filled my eyes.

"Robert," I shared, "You've made this day and the memory of your Mother and your birth very special for me. I'm so honored and touched that you took the time to find me. Not everyone would have done this. I can see that you loved your mom very dearly. This visit was a marvelous tribute to her."

Now it was my turn. I stood, holding his hands. Robert quickly followed my lead and stood. I looked up with an understanding smile. Perched on my tiptoes, I reached under his arms and across his back. I drew him in and gave Robert a big hug–a hug every mother would understand.

Made in the USA
San Bernardino, CA
20 August 2014